# Personal Ensign

# Personal Ensign

*by* BILL HELLER

THOROUGHBRED
**Legends**®
No. 11

Lexington, Kentucky

Library of Congress Control Number: 2001090247

ISBN 1-58150-060-2

Printed in The United States
First Edition: September 2001

a division of
The Blood-Horse, Inc.
PUBLISHERS SINCE 1916

To learn more about Personal Ensign
and other classic Thoroughbreds, see:

www.thoroughbredlegends.com

# Personal Ensign

# Contents

## *Impressions*

S ecluded in the northeastern corner of the Oklahoma Training Track, Barn 81 is far removed from the commotion of the famous racetrack across Union Avenue in Saratoga Springs, New York.

Halfway down the shed row on a lazy August morning in 2000, Ogden Phipps, the ninety-one-year-old patriarch of one of racing's most famous families, sits quietly in a director's chair watching horses cool out on the lawn separating trainer Shug McGaughey's barn from the rest of civilization otherwise known as East Avenue.

Phipps' eyesight is greatly diminished. His clarity of mind and love of horses not a bit.

Nearby, Phipps' son, Dinny, keeps watch at the gap as dozens of Thoroughbreds walk onto the training track or jog past him. In one hand is the leash of his dog, Danny. In the other, the ever-present cigar, almost as symbolic as the famed black and cherry silks his family's horses have been racing in for more than seven decades.

McGaughey walks toward the elder Phipps.

"Good morning, Mr. Phipps."

"How are you, Shug?"

As they chat under the shed row protected from the hot August sun, the years slowly seem to melt away.

Could it be a dozen years since they watched their undefeated four-year-old filly Personal Ensign standing in a tub of water on that same lawn the day after defeating colts in the Whitney Handicap?

"We ran her in the Whitney and she hit herself," McGaughey said. "And her leg blew up a little bit. Remember, Mr. Phipps? We used to stand her in a tub right out there. I'd stand her in warm water and Epsom salts."

Caution and patience are the linchpins of their stable, and no horse deserved them more than Personal Ensign, who had come back from a fractured pastern as a two-year-old to continue her career. The injury would have retired just about any other Thoroughbred.

"She was a hell of a filly," Phipps said, smiling at the memory. "She had a great heart. And she tried every time."

Her timing was impeccable. She not only measured

Winning Colors to take the 1988 Breeders' Cup Distaff later that year by a nose, a phenomenal performance which allowed her to retire as the first undefeated American champion in eighty years, but she also resurrected one of racing's most storied stables.

Seventy-five years earlier Ogden Phipps' mother, Gladys, and his uncle, Ogden Mills, had begun racing Thoroughbreds as Wheatley Stable and triggered a love affair with horses that has endured for generations, producing a steady stream of major stakes winners. But in 1984, Ogden Phipps was struggling. He had been racing his own horses for fifty-three years, but that year they had won just four races. That same year, he bred his mare, Grecian Banner, to his stallion Private Account. Phipps named the resulting filly Personal Ensign. She made an unremarkable first impression.

In 1986 Personal Ensign and a handful of other homebreds arrived at the track just as McGaughey was beginning his tenure as the Phipps family's trainer. McGaughey shared the same high regard for Thoroughbreds and their welfare and of doing what is best for the horse.

Personal Ensign's perfect record heading into the

1988 Distaff at Churchill Downs was a tribute to McGaughey, the son of a Lexington, Kentucky, dry cleaner who used to sneak into Keeneland as an adolescent; Dr. Larry Bramlage, the veterinarian who mended her broken pastern so well in 1986 that she was able to race again; and Randy Romero, the jockey who rode her in all but one start and who somehow survived a horrific accident in the jockeys' room, which nearly burned his entire body.

In that 1988 Distaff, a race many call the greatest in Breeders' Cup history, Personal Ensign's cause seemed hopeless. Staring down the length of the Churchill Downs stretch, on a muddy track she was clearly struggling to handle, she went after front-running Winning Colors, who seemed to have an insurmountable advantage. In the final frantic yards, Personal Ensign lunged forward, beating Winning Colors by inches to conclude a perfect career.

Maybe people overrate first impressions. Maybe it's the last impression that lives forever in our minds.

*Bill Heller*
*Albany, New York, 2001*

# PERSONAL ENSIGN

# CHAPTER 1

## *Generations*

T horoughbred racing might not have witnessed the career of an undefeated filly in the 1980s, nor enjoyed the impact and leadership of three generations of the Phipps family were it not for Gladys Livingston Mills, an avid rider and horsewoman who in 1907 married Henry Carnegie Phipps.

Gladys, along with her polo-playing husband, and her brother, Ogden L. Mills, who would become Secretary of the Treasury in Herbert Hoover's administration, established Wheatley Stable. The stable's immense success lasted for decades and has been mirrored by Gladys and Henry's son, Ogden Phipps, and their grandchildren, Ogden Mills (Dinny) and Cynthia. Collectively, the Phipps family has bred more than 250 stakes winners that have accounted for more than 750 stakes victories.

"They're kind of like the last of the Mohicans," said Seth Hancock, whose family's Claiborne Farm has been handling the breeding stock of the Phipps family for three decades. "They're one of the only truly private stables left. They're not commercial in any aspect. They've managed to flourish doing it that way, and I think that's been remarkable."

Henry Carnegie Phipps was the fourth of five children. His father, Henry Phipps, became friends with Andrew Carnegie during their boyhood in Pittsburgh. As sons of Scottish immigrants, they shared the same heritage. When Carnegie bought a piece of the Kloman steel forge in 1861, he gave his friend Phipps, then a twenty-two-year-old cobbler, a half-interest in exchange for eight hundred dollars and bookkeeping duties. Kloman became Carnegie Steel, which morphed into U.S. Steel, and Phipps' eight hundred dollars turned into a family fortune that has flourished for more than a century.

Phipps, a dapper man with a well-trimmed beard and spectacles, used part of his fortune for philanthropy, giving the city of Pittsburgh the Phipps Conservatory and Botanical Gardens, a magnificent palace that cost

$110,000 to build. It opened in 1893, and on January 1, 2001, was merged with the Pittsburgh Garden Place and renamed the Phipps Garden Center.

Phipps also contributed heavily to Johns Hopkins Hospital in Baltimore, allowing it to open the nation's first inpatient facility for the mentally ill. The Phipps Building honors his memory.

Wanting to guarantee a secure future for his family, Phipps established the Bessemer Trust Company, a trust and securities firm that today manages the $6.5 billion Phipps estate as well as the assets of other wealthy families and individuals.

Henry Phipps had little interest in horse racing, but his son, Henry Carnegie, certainly did. This interest fanned considerably when he married Gladys.

"She loved her horses," their son, Ogden Phipps, said. "And she would be there (at the racetrack) all the time."

A photograph taken when Ogden Phipps was six shows him at the racetrack, resting his chin on the rail, a smile on his face. Gladys is sitting next to him, her hands folded over the rail, one of them holding a program. She is wearing a large plumed hat. Another picture, taken many years later, shows her leading Bold

Ruler and jockey Eddie Arcaro into the winner's circle after a stakes victory at Belmont Park.

Ogden Phipps' son, Dinny, also knows how much his grandmother enjoyed racing and was partners with her on several horses. "I was very close with my grandmother," he said. "She knew everything about her horses. She consulted with Bull Hancock or his father on matings the same way we do today with Seth, but she had the final decision. She was an extraordinary lady."

Gladys Phipps bought her first three yearlings in 1925 at the Saratoga sales, paying "about $8,000" for the most expensive one, Potent, Ogden Phipps told Tim Capps in a 1988 story in *Spur*. Her horses raced under Wheatley Stable, the name taken from the highway bordering her Long Island estate. The next year she bought eight more yearlings from Harry Payne Whitney, the country's leading breeder seven times and leading owner six times.

"She bought four of the Whitney yearlings for $3,500 apiece and the other four for $5,000," Ogden Phipps said in a 1989 *New York Times* story by Steve Crist. "There were four stakes winners of the eight. Quite a start."

Wheatley Stable's trainer, Sunny Jim Fitzsimmons,

had picked them all. A couple of years earlier he had become trainer for another bastion of the Turf, William Woodward's Belair Stable. Fitzsimmons sent out the Triple Crown-winning father-son duo of Gallant Fox and Omaha for Woodward. When Dinny Phipps won his first race as an owner with Medici in 1962, Fitzsimmons, who trained for the Phipps family for thirty-eight years, said to Dinny, "I won that for you as well as for your grandmother and your father."

For Wheatley, Fitzsimmons got off to a quick start. Dice, one of the Whitney yearlings he had picked out, became a champion two-year-old of 1927 with four stakes wins, including the Keene Memorial, Juvenile, and Great American, before dying that same year. Nixie captured the 1928 Test and Alabama Stakes. Distraction won the 1928 Wood Memorial and was third in the 1930 Suburban Handicap. Diavolo won the 1927 Tremont Stakes and was third in the 1928 Belmont Stakes. In 1929 he won eight of eleven starts, including the Saratoga, Dixie, and Brookdale handicaps and Saratoga, Pimlico, and Jockey Club Gold cups.

Wheatley Stable's purple and gold silks would be known at every major racetrack in the country, even

though one of the best horses Gladys Phipps ever bred did his best after being sold to Charles S. Howard. That horse was Seabiscuit.

Among the ninety-three stakes winners raced by Wheatley Stable were ten champions, including Dice, Diavolo, High Voltage, Misty Morn, Bold Lad, Successor, and the great Bold Ruler.

Bold Ruler had a tremendous impact not only on the Phippses, but also on Thoroughbred racing and breeding. Bred by Wheatley Stable, Bold Ruler was a standout on the racetrack before he became a standout in the breeding shed. A top two-year-old of 1956, he went into his three-year-old season a leading contender for the Kentucky Derby. Although he finished a disappointing fourth in that race, he rebounded to take the Preakness Stakes, then put together a remarkable fall campaign to earn champion three-year-old and Horse of the Year honors.

Bold Ruler was produced from Wheatley Stable's stakes-winning mare Miss Disco, who was named the 1958 Kentucky Broodmare of the Year for her son's accomplishments, and was sired by the imported English stallion Nasrullah, a five-time leading sire in the

United States. Nasrullah, who led the list for the last time in 1962, was replaced in that lofty position the following year by his son Bold Ruler, who would lead America's sire list from 1963 through 1969 and again in 1973.

In 1964 Wheatley Stable became leading owner for the first time with earnings of $1,073,572. However, the zenith of Wheatley Stable's success occurred in 1966, when it again finished as the number one owner in the country, this time with earnings of $1,225,861.

Twenty-two years later Ogden Phipps, who inherited his passion for racing from his mother, would finish number one as both an owner and breeder for the first of two consecutive years.

Ogden Phipps was born on November 26, 1908, in New York City. After graduating from St. Paul's in New Hampshire, he attended Harvard. Upon his graduation in 1931, he worked at Smith Barney before taking over the chairmanship of Bessemer Trust Company.

In addition to his career in finance, Phipps incorporated breeding and racing as serious pursuits and has been ably carrying the family's racing banner since the mid-1930s.

He wed Lillian Bostwick in 1937, and they made their home in Roslyn, Long Island. The marriage unit-

ed two of the most socially prominent racing families in New York. Lillian's brother George "Pete" Bostwick was a renowned polo player and steeplechase rider and was inducted into racing's Hall of Fame in 1968. Another brother, Dunbar Bostwick, was vice president and treasurer of Saratoga Harness, the track across the street from Saratoga Race Course. Lillian Phipps raced her own stable of steeplechase horses, none better than three-time champion Neji.

Ogden Phipps would become one of Thoroughbred racing's spokesmen and leaders in a variety of capacities. He was elected to The Jockey Club at the age of thirty. Twenty-six years later he was named the sixth chairman of The Jockey Club.

Acting as vice chairman of The Jockey Club, Phipps, in 1953, appointed Captain Harry Guggenheim, John W. Hanes, and Christopher T. Chenery to a committee to jump-start racing in New York. That committee created the Greater New York Racing Association, Inc., the predecessor of the New York Racing Association, which operates Saratoga, Belmont Park, and Aqueduct. Ogden Phipps is now a trustee emeritus of the association he helped form.

Professionally, Ogden Phipps would serve on the board of directors of Texaco and International Paper and serve as a trustee of New York Hospital and a director of St. Barnabas's Hospital. But the love of his life has always been horses.

Ogden Phipps registered his now famous black and cherry cap colors in 1932. His son Dinny's nearly identical colors are black, cherry collar, cuffs, and cap. His daughter, Cynthia, chose the gold and purple her grandmother had used for Wheatley Stable.

Racing a modest-sized stable, Ogden Phipps won his first stakes in 1935 with White Cockade in the Youth Stakes. Another of his early stars was King Cole. As a three-year-old in 1941, King Cole finished second to Triple Crown winner Whirlaway in the Preakness as Phipps' first horse to compete in a Triple Crown race.

Phipps was a competitive athlete himself — in court tennis. Court tennis is the ancestor of modern tennis known as "royal tennis" in Australia and as "real tennis" in the United Kingdom, where it is more popular than in the United States. He was the U.S. National Court Tennis Champion from 1934 through 1937 and in 1948 and '49. He was also British Champion in 1949.

From January 1942 through 1946, Phipps served in the Navy, retiring with the rank of commander in the Reserves. His naval experience supplied him with a stream of nautical names for his Thoroughbreds, including Personal Ensign, Personal Flag, and Polish Navy. From the first letters of his naval assignment in the Bureau of Supplies and Accounts, he came up with Busanda, his 1950 Alabama Stakes winner who would have a profound influence on future Phipps runners.

His mother's more powerful Wheatley Stable and Bold Ruler often overshadowed the racing stable of Ogden Phipps. Yet, Ogden Phipps occasionally benefited from Bold Ruler's genes in such outstanding performers as Queen of the Stage, Reviewer, Our Hero, and Vitriolic.

From 1970 through 1979, Bold Ruler's descendants won seven Kentucky Derbys, but none were for Ogden Phipps, who has had only four Kentucky Derby starters. Dapper Dan was second by a neck to Lucky Debonair in the 1965 Derby before running second again by the same margin to Tom Rolfe in the Preakness. Easy Goer, the 1988 champion two-year-old colt, was second in both the Kentucky Derby and Preakness the following year to Sunday Silence before blowing him away in the Belmont Stakes by eight lengths, giving Phipps his only Triple Crown race victory in fourteen starts.

Buckpasser might have given him another classic victory had he been healthy enough to run. Voted champion two-year-old colt in 1965 after winning nine of eleven starts, Buckpasser missed the entire Triple Crown after developing a quarter crack while training for the Florida Derby. Buckpasser returned to extend his winning streak to twelve with victories in the Travers, Woodward, Lawrence Realization, and Jockey Club Gold Cup, and was named not only champion three-year-old colt but 1966 Horse of the Year, too. His win streak reached fifteen the next year before he ran third to Poker in the Bowling Green Handicap, Buckpasser's lone start on grass. Though plagued by quarter cracks and the onset of arthritis in his right front hoof and pastern, Buckpasser still accomplished enough to be named 1967 champion handicap horse. To honor his outstanding runner, Ogden Phipps named his gigantic yacht *Buckpasser*.

Phipps might have raced a Triple Crown winner had he lost the flip of a coin. Well after Bold Ruler had

established himself as a dominant stallion, Phipps and his mother devised a foal-sharing arrangement that allowed breeders of top mares an alternative to paying a stud fee. A breeder with a qualified mare could breed to Bold Ruler for two seasons, with the breeder getting one foal and the Phippses the other. When Christopher Chenery sent his mare Somethingroyal to Bold Ruler, she produced a filly and then a colt. Chenery and Phipps tossed a coin to decide who got which foal. Phipps won the flip and selected the first of the two foals, The Bride, a filly who raced four times, never finishing better than sixth. She did, however, produce three stakes horses for the Phippses. Chenery got stuck with Secretariat. "Flipping a coin was Chenery's idea not mine," Phipps told Crist in 1989. "He thought it would be more fun."

It was. For Chenery.

Phipps missed out on Secretariat, but long before Secretariat won the Triple Crown in 1973, Phipps made a crucial decision that paved the way for decades of continued success and the birth of an undefeated filly.

# CHAPTER 2

## *Building A Stable*

T he genesis of Phipps' spectacular success in racing, as well as the breeding of Personal Ensign and her full brother Personal Flag, traces back to mares Ogden Phipps purchased from the dispersal sale of Colonel E.R. Bradley's estate in 1946. Bradley, who owned Idle Hour Stock Farm near Lexington, Kentucky, had assembled an exceptional band of broodmares that produced a seemingly never ending arsenal of stakes winners. Bradley bred and raced four Kentucky Derby winners: Behave Yourself (1921), Bubbling Over (1926), Burgoo King (1932), and Brokers Tip (1933).

Phipps was part of a syndicate that included Robert Kleberg of King Ranch and John Hay Whitney and Joan Payson of Greentree Stud. The syndicate purchased Bradley's racing and breeding stock for a reported three million dollars. The three members chose twelve to eighteen horses apiece and sold the rest to Edward S. Moore, Charles S. Howard, and Maine Chance Farm.

Phipps bought five broodmares, including Bloodroot, Businesslike, and Baby League, plus four yearlings and three weanlings. Three of the mares Phipps purchased were daughters of the great French broodmare La Troienne. "Every one of my grade I stakes winners in 1988 had that La Troienne blood," Phipps said in a story in *The New York Times*.

Bloodroot, who produced stakes winners Bric a Brac, Be Faithful, and Bimlette, was Kentucky's first Broodmare of the Year, chosen in 1946 by the Thoroughbred Breeders of Kentucky, the forerunner of the Kentucky Thoroughbred Owners and Breeders. After receiving the award, she foaled Ancestor, Mrs. Ogden Phipps' 1959 steeplechase champion.

Two of the daughters of La Troienne, Businesslike and Baby League, made the most significant contribution to the Phipps racing and breeding program. Businesslike, by Blue Larkspur, was in foal to War Admiral at the time of the purchase. The following year she produced Busanda, who would go on to win the 1950 Alabama Stakes under the Phipps colors.

Like her half sister Businesslike, Baby League (by Bubbling Over) was also in foal to Triple Crown winner War Admiral at the time of her purchase. She, too, produced a filly, named Striking, who would go on to win the 1949 Schuylerville Stakes for Phipps.

These three quarter sisters were even better as broodmares. When Busanda was bred in 1962 to Tom Fool, a grandson of Hyperion's half brother Pharamond II, she had already produced two minor stakes winners in Bupers and Bureaucracy, but this union was to bring about her greatest achievement. The following year she foaled a bay colt that was to make headlines on the sports pages of newspapers across the country, multiple champion and Horse of the Year Buckpasser. At stud Buckpasser sired thirty-five stakes winners, including La Prevoyante, Numbered Account, and Relaxing. He was the broodmare sire of 142 stakes winners, including eleven champions.

Although Busanda had the greater success on the racetrack, Striking far surpassed her in the breeding shed. Her sons and daughters might not have achieved the prominence of a Buckpasser, but she did produce five stakes winners: the appropriately named Hitting Away,

Bases Full, Batter Up, My Boss Lady, and Glamour. Striking was named Broodmare of the Year, largely from the performances of her son and daughter Hitting Away and Batter Up.

Carrying the La Troienne blood into a new generation, Glamour, a daughter of Nasrullah, won the Jasmine Stakes and the prestigious Test Stakes at Saratoga in 1956. In 1963 Phipps decided to breed her to Kentucky Derby winner Swaps, a grandson of the great sire Hyperion.

Although not the caliber of Buckpasser, the Swaps—Glamour foal, named Intriguing, would be a useful enough runner. The chestnut filly placed in three stakes at two, her only year on the racetrack. In 1968 she was bred to her somewhat distant kinsman in blood, Buckpasser, who had recently been retired to the historic stud barn of Claiborne Farm. On April 8, 1969, their bay filly, Numbered Account, struggled to her feet in a straw-bedded stall. She would become a champion two-year-old filly.

Numbered Account debuted in mid May of 1971, winning by ten lengths. Five days later she returned to win her first stakes effort, the Fashion Stakes, coming from far off the pace in a manner that was reminiscent of her sire, Buckpasser. Her only loss among her division was in the Adirondack Stakes at Saratoga. She then reeled off consecutive victories in the Spinaway, Matron, Frizette, Selima, and Gardenia stakes. She would lose only once more at two, finishing fourth against colts in the Garden State Stakes. She concluded her championship season with eight victories in ten starts and earnings of $446,594. She went on to win six more races in twelve starts at three and four, equaling a track record in the Spinster Stakes as a three-year-old. She retired with fourteen wins and total earnings of $607,048.

Whether by design or chance, the descendants of the two most important Phipps purchases from the Bradley estate traveled on parallel paths: the blood of La Troienne in the female family mated to scions of the great sire-producing matriarch Selene, dam of both Hyperion and Pharamond II.

By this time Phipps was surely aware of the magnitude of his good fortune from the purchase of the descendants of La Troienne from the Bradley estate. However, it was not only for him that Bradley's bloodlines had been so successful, but for the other original syndicate members as well. From this dispersal Greentree Stud had acquired the broodmare Blade of Time, a daughter of

Sickle—Bar Nothing, by Blue Larkspur. Blade of Time would become the granddam of the brilliant Damascus, who earned his fame in the white with red polka dot silks of Mrs. Thomas Bancroft.

Damascus was a son of the bright chestnut stallion Sword Dancer, who, like his son after him, was Horse of the Year and a descendant of the Teddy line, which, at that time, was teetering on the brink of extinction. Damascus' dam was Kerala, a daughter of My Babu and Blade of Time, whom Mrs. Bancroft had purchased as a yearling. Greentree Stud had consigned Kerala through Duval Headley to the Keeneland summer sale.

From a select list of stallions at Claiborne, Phipps opted for Damascus as a mate for his prize filly Numbered Account in 1975. The choice might be seen as a measure of respect on Phipps' part since Damascus had soundly beaten his Buckpasser in the 1967 Woodward Stakes, thereby giving the three-year-old the Horse of the Year title.

The following spring Numbered Account foaled a bay colt that would become both a solid racehorse and sire for Phipps. Private Account won six of thirteen starts and earned $339,396 during two seasons of racing. He counted among his wins the grade I Widener and Gulfstream Park handicaps and the grade II Jim Dandy Stakes. He entered stud at Claiborne Farm in 1981 and went on to sire sixty stakes winners, including Inside Information, East of the Moon, and Private Terms. He was pensioned from stud duty in 1995 and is living out his life at Claiborne.

In 1963 Phipps decided to add to his broodmare band with several outside mares. They included the top English mare Aunt Edith II, who produced stakes winners My Great Aunt and Critical Cousin; 1966 champion three-year-old filly Lady Pitt, whom the Phippses purchased after her racing career; and Dorine, a star in South America.

Dorine would produce Grecian Banner, the dam of Personal Ensign and Personal Flag. "I bought several expensive mares, but the one I wanted the most, Dorine, was really not very expensive," Phipps told Tim Capps in the story in *Spur*. "In South America, she was something, the greatest. You ask [trainers] Angel Penna or Horatio Luro about her and they throw up their hands in exclamation."

Dorine was a daughter of Aristophanes, the sire of

Forli, who was undefeated in Argentina and sired three-time Horse of the Year Forego. Dorine's dam, Doria, won eleven stakes in Argentina in the early 1950s. In a 1988 story in *The Blood-Horse*, Edward L. Bowen wrote that Doria was regarded as one of the best sprinters in Argentinian history.

Dorine won eleven of twenty-one starts and earned $151,027, retiring in 1963 as Argentina's all-time leading money-winning mare.

Ogden Phipps acquired Dorine after she had produced four foals. She was purchased in foal to Martial and sent to Claiborne Farm in Kentucky, where the Phipps family has long boarded its mares. The Martial foal was named Law and Order and never raced.

Phipps then bred Dorine to Bold Ruler, and she produced a stakes winner named Our Hero, who earned more than $175,000. Dorine was next sent to Mrs. Stephen C. Clark Jr.'s brilliant Hoist the Flag. This phenomenal colt, a son of Tom Rolfe out of the War Admiral mare Wavy Navy, finished first in all six of his starts, but was disqualified in one of them, the Champagne Stakes at two. He also captured the 1970 Cowdin Stakes and earned the two-year-old championship. He won his three-year-old debut in allowance company by fifteen lengths, then the Bay Shore Stakes by seven in a sparkling 1:21 for seven furlongs.

While preparing for the Kentucky Derby, Hoist the Flag shattered his pastern. Surgery saved his life, and he was sent to the stud barn. He went on to sire Alleged, Sensational, Linkage, and forty-eight other stakes winners before dying in 1980.

Dorine's Hoist the Flag foal was a filly, Grecian Banner. Born in 1974, Grecian Banner won just one of six starts and a meager $9,020. Phipps first bred Grecian Banner to his homebred stallion Private Account in 1981 and got the winning filly Personal Colors. The following year Grecian Banner was sent back to Private Account and the resulting foal, a colt, was named Personal Flag, who went on to win the grade I Suburban and Widener handicaps and earn over a million dollars.

In 1983 Grecian Banner, who would be named Kentucky Broodmare of the Year five years later, was bred to Private Account for the third straight time. The dark bay foal she delivered on April 27, 1984, was Personal Ensign.

The birth of Personal Ensign would herald a new era for the Phipps family stable whose racing magic had suddenly seemed to disappear. In 1984 Ogden Phipps' horses won just four races and $106,620. Wheatley Stable, Ogden Phipps, and his wife Lillian, had amassed seventeen championships from 1950 through 1971, but few afterward. Mrs. Phipps' Straight and True was named the champion steeplechaser of 1976. Ogden Phipps' great mare Relaxing was champion handicap mare in 1981. Cynthia Phipps raced the 1982 three-year-old filly champion Christmas Past. There were no others.

Then Shug McGaughey joined the team.

# PERSONAL ENSIGN

## CHAPTER 3

# *Shug*

Claude R. "Shug" McGaughey III was born January 6, 1951, in Lexington, Kentucky, but not into a world of Thoroughbreds. His family was in the laundry and dry-cleaning business, an endeavor his dad grew tired of before venturing into real estate.

Although McGaughey doesn't know how he came to be called Shug, nicknames abound in his family. His grandfather, Claude, was known as Mack. His father, Claude Jr., got labeled Dooney, which was the closest his baby sister could come to pronouncing Junior.

McGaughey guesses he was twelve or thirteen the first time his dad took him to Keeneland. They'd go once in the spring and once in the fall, and it wasn't long until McGaughey was going on his own after school, even though he really didn't have the money to do so. "I was kind of taken over by the (racing) bug a little bit," he said.

He and his friends would sneak into Keeneland. McGaughey would look for discarded pages from the *Daily Racing Form*. "I'd pick up the *Racing Form* from the people who had taken out just the Keeneland PPs [past performance lines] and bring the rest of it home," he said. "I'd read the articles and maybe look at the horses that were running at Arlington. It sort of evolved from there."

When he did have a few dollars to bring to the track, his betting strategy was simple. "We'd try to hit the [daily] double to keep going the rest of the day," he said.

While he was in high school, McGaughey began working on the fringes of the industry, toiling briefly on the farm crew at famed Calumet. McGaughey also attended horse shows. "Walt Robertson, who's one of the heads of Fasig-Tipton, his brother had show horses, and they took me around to the horse shows when I was seventeen or eighteen, to places like Harrodsburg, Kentucky; Danville; and the state fair in Louisville," McGaughey said. Then McGaughey worked at Saddlebred auctions at Tattersalls in Lexington, taking sales slips to be signed and returning receipts to bidders.

The more involved he became with the horse industry, the more he loved it. But he went to college at the University of Mississippi, with the intent of majoring in business — and lasted for two years. "That was the first year they had the (Vietnam) draft lottery, and I drew a high number, so I asked my parents, 'Can I take a semester off?' " McGaughey said. "They said, 'Yeah, but you have to get a job.' "

His parents didn't have to ask him where he wanted to work.

The brother-in-law of one of McGaughey's friends, Sammy Cottrell, was David Carr, a trainer who had a stable of eight to ten horses at Keeneland. McGaughey signed on to a seven-day workweek for forty dollars and the long hours and low pay didn't bother him in the least. "I think I became enthralled with the whole atmosphere," he said. "I mean I really enjoyed it. I enjoyed being around the barn. I enjoyed the after hours of it. When the work was done in the morning, I'd like to hang around and straighten up and rake up, even when I was just a hotwalker. Make sure the laundry was right."

McGaughey's work ethic and attention to detail served him well, along with his willingness to learn.

"They (the other workers) were teaching me, and I was intrigued," McGaughey told Randy Moss in a 1984

*Derby* magazine article. "If anything had to be done, I always wanted to be there to watch. I was always looking over the veterinarian's shoulder. I felt that if ever I had to do it myself, I wouldn't want anyone standing over my shoulder and telling me what to do. I wanted to be able to make those decisions by myself."

McGaughey spent two years as a groom for Carr, witnessing the brilliant two-year-old filly La Prevoyante finish her perfect twelve-for-twelve juvenile season by winning the Gardenia Stakes at Garden State Park in 1972. Then he saw Secretariat take the Garden State Stakes a week later on the way to becoming the first two-year-old Horse of the Year.

"That'll get your blood going. I'd never been around horses like that," McGaughey said in 2001.

McGaughey accompanied the Carr stable on a circuit that also included Liberty Bell near Philadelphia, Keeneland, Latonia (now Turfway Park), and Sportsman's Park in Chicago. Then he caught on with a bigger stable run by Jimmy Cowden, a friend of McGaughey's dad who had a thirty-five-horse stable with some decent horses, including some claimers and well-bred maidens.

McGaughey spent nine months with Cowden and moved on after learning from Turf writer Jobie Arnold that John Fulton, who trained for New York Yankees owner George Steinbrenner's Kinsman Stable, needed help. McGaughey got a job as a groom and worked with Fulton through the Keeneland fall meet before spending the winter with him in Florida.

At a Yankees exhibition baseball game in Florida, Steinbrenner offered McGaughey work on his farm in Ocala. McGaughey accepted, but quickly realized he far preferred the racetrack. He remained with Kinsman, but at Monmouth Park. Later, when Fulton couldn't get stalls at Keeneland because of Steinbrenner's trouble with illegal campaign contributions, McGaughey had to make a choice. "He wanted us all to go back to the farm in Ocala until he got all that straightened out," McGaughey said. "That was the last place in the world I wanted to go back to."

McGaughey spoke with a friend, Mike Bell, who worked for top trainer Frank Whiteley. Bell told McGaughey, "You need to come work here." McGaughey leapt at the opportunity.

McGaughey landed a job with Whiteley in

November of 1973, working in Camden, South Carolina, where Whiteley wintered his horses. "I worked there all winter with the babies, rubbing horses, and then I sort of moved up to where I was taking care of a barn after I'd been there a couple of months," McGaughey said.

That was after Frank Whiteley advised McGaughey to get out of the business. McGaughey retold the conversation:

"Frank said to me, 'You really like this, don't you?' "

"Yeah, I do."

"Well, I advised my son [David] to do something else. [David didn't take his father's advice.] For every good thing that happens, twenty bad things are going to happen."

"I said, 'I'll take that, because I'm going to stick around for a while.' "

When Whiteley shipped four horses to New York in March of 1975, McGaughey went with them. David Whiteley, who normally would have handled the quartet, was in California with other horses in the Whiteley stable. When David Whiteley returned to New York, he made McGaughey his assistant.

"McGaughey was a breath of fresh air," David Whiteley told Moss in his interview. "We were on the same wavelength. You never really had to tell him what to do. He knew what to do."

It was an exciting time to be with the Whiteleys. Ruffian, owned by Ogden Phipps' sister and brother-in-law Barbara and Stuart Janney, was undefeated and on the way to compiling her own perfect record. Tragically, she had to be put down after she broke both her sesamoids during a match race with 1975 Kentucky Derby winner Foolish Pleasure. "That was pretty tough," McGaughey said. When asked how Frank Whiteley got through her devastating death, McGaughey said, "He's a pretty tough guy. He felt like he had to set an example for the rest of the barn." McGaughey added that the addition of Forego to the Whiteley Stable several months later helped the trainer a great deal.

Other top horses caught McGaughey's eye in New York, particularly the ones belonging to the Phippses. "I remember walking out of the backstretch gate and I was walking by the Phipps barn. I was in awe," McGaughey said. "I wouldn't go in it, but I looked down the shed on the end. Even sometimes when I'd see them school

horses, I'd walk up to the paddock just to look at them. I was in awe of the whole thing."

McGaughey spent four and a half years with the Whiteleys, from the fall of 1974 through the spring of 1979.

McGaughey was with a string of the Whiteley horses in California in the winter of 1978-79 when he spent five or six days with two good friends, Bill O'Neil and Reynolds Bell, Mike Bell's brother. They told McGaughey that through a program for new and prospective owners called A Day in Kentucky, they had met neophyte owners Pat and Anne Dunnigan. In fact, O'Neil and Bell left California to meet with the Dunnigans in Abilene, Texas, where the couple had a farm and training center. The Dunnigans had just purchased a farm in Kentucky and were beginning to invest good money in well-bred yearlings.

"I remember, it was either a Saturday or Sunday afternoon," McGaughey said. "We (the Whiteley team) were running Tiller in the Santa Anita Handicap. He'd finished second to Affirmed, and we came back to the barn and the phone rings and it was them (O'Neil and Bell)."

McGaughey figured O'Neil and Bell were curious about Tiller's race because they had been hanging around the Whiteley barn. Instead, his friends told him

that not only was the Dunnigan family deeply interest-
ed in racing, but they might have a job available for
McGaughey. O'Neil told McGaughey, "We've got these
people very interested. They've got a few horses in
California and they maybe want to have some in the
East. Would you be interested in talking to them?"

Hell yes.

"They [the Dunnigans] came out there the next weekend, and I remember we ate dinner on a Saturday night,"
McGaughey said. "They were pretty green. They bought a
bunch of nice fillies, pedigree fillies. He wanted to get into the
business big, so we talked, me and Pat and his wife, Anne."

That Monday morning, McGaughey's phone rang
again. It was Pat Dunnigan.

"If you want the job, it's yours."

"Well, I want it."

McGaughey was a head trainer at the age of twen-
ty-eight. "At that time, I thought I knew everything,"
McGaughey said. "I thought, 'Oh, boy, I'm ready to
go!' I knew nothing, until I got the horses. When
you're working under somebody, you don't know
quite as much as you think you know. Then you've got
to learn all over again. But you have your basics."

McGaughey had his start. And he made the most out of his opportunity, racing the Dunnigan horses, under the stable name Bacacita Farms, and a couple of other horses at Rockingham Park in New Hampshire. McGaughey's first winner was a maiden $10,000 claimer nicknamed "Big John," who was owned by his friend Joe Allen.

McGaughey spent the next two years racing at Rockingham, Keeneland and Churchill Downs, Arlington Park outside Chicago, and Oaklawn Park in Hot Springs, Arkansas. It did not take people long to realize the young trainer had a pretty good idea of what he was doing as his numbers jumped up quickly. In 1979 he had three wins, three seconds, and two thirds from twenty starts and earnings of $23,329. In 1980 he posted eighteen wins, sixteen seconds, and fifteen thirds in eighty-five starts and earnings of $193,448.

McGaughey arrived at Oaklawn Park for the 1981 spring meet with a dozen horses, all but one a filly, and most of them untested maidens. "It was the first time I'd ever had a decent amount of horses to work with," he said. "I was anxious to see how I'd make out."

Here's how: Eight of the first nine horses he saddled

won. He finished the meet with thirteen wins in just twenty-four starts. "We made a big hit," McGaughey said. McGaughey finished 1981 with twenty-two wins, fifteen seconds, and twelve thirds from ninety-nine starts and earnings of $283,516.

Then Pat Dunnigan died in February of 1982. "He had a heart attack on a treadmill," McGaughey said. "The horses were all left in trust to the children, who were underage. These guys, the trust officers, they didn't know anything about it. They were into banking and the oil and gas business."

Anne Dunnigan decided to keep a small stable in California and told McGaughey she wasn't going to buy any new horses. McGaughey didn't see much of a future in that, and he gave up the Dunnigan horses, which wound up in the capable hands of D. Wayne Lukas. Lukas and McGaughey's paths were destined to cross many, many times.

McGaughey retreated to Kentucky in September of 1982 and tried to piece together a small stable. "I had two horses," McGaughey said. "One of them belonged partly to me and the other belonged to Billy O'Neil. And we got going from there. A few of my friends helped me

a little bit, Reynolds and Mike Bell's uncle, John Bell, David Greathouse, Tommy Roach, and Ron Kirk. Tommy Roach gave me horses and fronted me money."

Nobody helped McGaughey more than another friend, Dr. Gary Lavin, a veterinarian who had pull with owner John Ed Anthony's powerful Loblolly Stables, then trained by Joe Cantey. When McGaughey wintered at Oaklawn Park and again did well, Lavin went to bat for him. "They had a lot of horses at the time, and John Ed Anthony felt they needed an outlet for the horses that wouldn't do in New York," McGaughey said. "So he sent me a bunch of horses to take back to Kentucky, and some of them were okay. And I had Lavin at the time, too, and along with these other people, they sort of helped me get going."

He had planted the seeds for his incredible 24.3 percent career winning percentage as well as an unfathomable 57.7 percent career in-the-money percentage through June of 2001 right at the start. And he did it the hard way those first few years, not benefiting from a single star to generate earnings. In fact, McGaughey didn't win a single black-type [stakes] race in 1979, '80, or '81. That would soon change.

Officially, McGaughey's first stakes winner was Northernette, who won the Apple Blossom Handicap at Oaklawn Park in 1978, but McGaughey was only deputizing for David Whiteley then.

McGaughey's first real stakes winner was Lavin's Party School, who won the Kentucky Stakes at Churchill Downs on May 29, 1982.

Befitting a trainer who would wind up handling the Phipps stable, which relies on top-performing fillies to become quality broodmares and produce a new generation of runners, McGaughey's best stakes horses in the early eighties were fillies.

John Bell's Try Something New won six stakes from 1982 to 1984, including McGaughey's first grade I victory, the 1983 Spinster at Keeneland.

Alan Samford's Lass Trump won five stakes in 1983 and '84, and made McGaughey's first foray to Saratoga a memorable one — his only previous starter at Saratoga had finished out of the money. Lass Trump won both the Test and Revidere Stakes in 1983 and then returned the following year to win the Ballerina. McGaughey's 1983 Saratoga meet could have been even better, had two of his best horses not lost photo

finishes by inches. Try Something New lost the Delaware Handicap by a nose to May Day Eighty, and Bold Style finished a nose behind Island Whirl in the Whitney Handicap.

Still, people noticed. How could they not?

Despite losing the Dunnigan horses, McGaughey watched his earnings leap-frog to $581,134 in 1982 and then more than double to $1,390,141 in 1983, when he posted sixty-seven wins, forty-one seconds, and thirty-nine thirds from just 230 starts.

In 1984 McGaughey started his first horses in the Kentucky Derby for Loblolly: Vanlandingham, who had won the $100,000 Rebel Stakes, and Pine Circle. The Loblolly entry went off at 6-1. Pine Circle overcame the eighteen post to finish sixth, seven and a quarter lengths behind the winner, Swale. Vanlandingham injured himself during the race, suffering a stress fracture of his cannon bone. He finished sixteenth in the field of twenty and was out of action for nearly thirteen months.

Even so, McGaughey's numbers continued to increase, as he won seventy-six races from 271 starts and earned more than two million dollars in 1984.

"The guy is something," Oaklawn trainer Terry

Brennan said at the time. "He deserves everything he gets, too, because he works harder than probably anybody on the backside."

Another trainer, Lynn Whiting, said, "Shug never sends out a short horse. He always has them in the right spots, and he never runs out of patience. I don't think he's long for the Midwest, in my opinion. I think he's headed for New York."

Vanlandingham tipped off McGaughey's talent of bringing horses back well prepared from long layoffs, winning an allowance race in 1985 at Churchill Downs by six lengths. Then Vanlandingham won the Stephen Foster Handicap by a half-length at Churchill Downs and the grade I Suburban Handicap by eight and three-quarter lengths at Belmont Park.

Sent off the even-money favorite in the grade I Whitney Handicap at Saratoga, Vanlandingham was bothered early and finished third behind Track Barron.

"I was stabled on the main track at Saratoga, and [Vanlandingham] had bad feet, and the main track just about wrecked him," McGaughey said. "It took him a long time to get over that."

But he did. Vanlandingham, on the way to being

named McGaughey's first champion as the 1985 older horse, finished second by four lengths to Track Barron in the Woodward Stakes and third by a length behind Chief's Crown and Gate Dancer in the Marlboro Cup, both grade I events at Belmont.

Vanlandingham's next start would be in another grade I stakes in New York, the Jockey Club Gold Cup. By then, McGaughey had reached the crossroads of his career.

"In 1985 I'd been up in Saratoga," McGaughey said. "I had some horses there and at Arlington and at Ellis Park. And when I left Saratoga, I said, 'I want to do something about this, because I don't like being all that spread out.' I kind of told myself, I said, 'You can either go back to Kentucky and have thirty-six horses around there and just be a trainer, or maybe try to put the best ones together and move to New York.' "

And then, again, McGaughey's phone rang one morning. It was Claiborne Farm president Seth Hancock, who asked McGaughey to come out to the farm that afternoon.

"He said the Phippses have called me, and they wanted to make a change (from trainer Angel Penna Sr.), and your name is on their list if you're interested," McGaughey recalled.

McGaughey didn't think twice: "I'm in."

In 2001 Hancock explained why he had recom-
mended McGaughey to the Phippses: "I've known
Shug for a long time. I've had a horse or two with him.
When Mr. Penna and the Phippses split up, I asked
Shug if he'd be interested. So I mentioned that to the
Phippses. I thought Shug was excellent with young
horses. He knew how to take one from the farm to the
starting gate of a racetrack, which is not something
everybody can do. I thought it would be a good fit.
Shug has a lot of class."

Though he might not have needed it, McGaughey got
a second recommendation from another old friend,
Warner Jones. "Warner Jones was a great trainer,"
Ogden Phipps said of the late master of Hermitage Farm.
"And he was a great friend of mine. He said Shug's the
man I should get. Seth Hancock said the same thing."

The Phippses pride themselves on being easy clients
to train horses for, and have entrusted their stable to
just a handful of conditioners. Sunny Jim Fitzsimmons
trained for them for thirty-eight years. He was followed in succession by Bill Winfrey, Eddie Neloy,
Roger Laurin, John Russell, and Angel Penna.

Fitzsimmons, Winfrey, Neloy, and Penna are all in the Hall of Fame. McGaughey will be after he clears the trainer's twenty-five-year minimum for eligibility.

Dinny Phipps explained one of McGaughey's talents. "The foundation of our racing stable is broodmares," he said. "And to be good broodmares, they have to perform on the racetrack. Some trainers are better training fillies. I'm not sure they'd say that, but it's a fact. In our operation, you have to be able to train fillies."

McGaughey could. Dinny Phipps set up a meeting with him at Dinny's house in Old Westbury, Long Island, the morning of the Jockey Club Gold Cup, when McGaughey would saddle Vanlandingham in a race in which Dinny Phipps, as The Jockey Club chairman, would be presenting the winning trophy.

McGaughey was more worried about the meeting than the race.

"I remember I was petrified going out there," McGaughey recalled. "You're going to sort of meet the unknown. These are very high-profile people with this very powerful racing stable, and I didn't know what to expect. It was raining as hard as it could rain. I rang the doorbell and Dinny opened the door. He's got a pair of khaki pants on and some boat shoes and a golf shirt and cigar. And he put me instantly at ease. We sat down in the den and we talked. We talked about ideas and training patterns, and how I like to do things, and personalities and this and that. They're very down-to-earth people. They're different away from the coats and ties."

That afternoon Vanlandingham won the Gold Cup, and Dinny Phipps presented McGaughey the trophy. How's that for a job interview?

Four days later, Dinny Phipps told McGaughey, "The job is yours."

Phipps said, "He was a first-rate trainer, and he represented the kind of quality person we wanted to be our trainer. He runs an honest stable. He works hard and he wants to win every race he goes in, and he wants to do it within the rules."

There were complications, none more painful to McGaughey than telling the owner of Loblolly Stable, John Ed Anthony, and a handful of other owners he trained for that he was going to leave. "Here I had gotten this job, but I had given up a nice stable of horses," McGaughey said. "John Ed Anthony was very, very

good to me. I think he was stunned. It was a very, very difficult thing for me to tell him."

When Anthony met McGaughey to see Carr de Naskra run in the Meadowlands Cup, he asked the trainer to stay on. "He asked me if I would think about reconsidering," McGaughey recalled. "I said, 'No.' "

"So I had gotten the job I wanted, but it was hard leaving the guy, among other people. Mr. [John] Bell is one of the greatest men that I've ever been associated with or been around in my life. The first grade I winner I had was for him, Try Something New. And he was a friend of mine. And there were others that were good to me. I gave up a lot."

He gained a lot, too.

# PERSONAL ENSIGN

## CHAPTER 4

## *New Surroundings*

S hug McGaughey didn't know what to expect from the well-bred yearlings that had recently been broken at Claiborne Farm and sent to the warmer climate of Ocala, Florida, to continue their education at Slew's Nest Farm.

He only knew that the Phipps' racing stable had undergone a down period. "I first saw the yearlings in December of their yearling year." McGaughey said. "I ate dinner with Mr. Phipps and spent the night at his house, and we flew the next morning up to Ocala from Palm Beach."

The Phippses sent their yearlings to Slew's Nest, a farm owned at the time by the Hills and Taylors of Seattle Slew fame, for their early training. When McGaughey inspected the new crop, the yearling he was most impressed with was not Personal Ensign, nor

Polish Navy, who would also be a star at two. "There was a full brother to Private Account there, by Damascus out of Numbered Account," McGaughey said. "I was more enthralled with him. He ended up getting hurt before he ever came to me. Polish Navy's mother (Navsup, who was winless in eleven starts and earned just four-thousand dollars) never had been anything, and I didn't know who Grecian Banner was."

McGaughey was heading into uncharted waters taking over the Phipps stable, but he wasn't going in alone. He enlisted his life-long friend, Buzz Tenney, as his assistant, a position Tenney has held ever since. Growing up in Lexington, McGaughey and Tenney were in the same Cub Scout troop, and both attended the University of Mississippi, though they went to different high schools.

"Buzz is kind of like the Phippses, the last assistant to stay where he is (rather than go out on his own), and I admire him for it," Seth Hancock said. "Part of it is loyalty. Most people in his spot have too big an ego. They have to show the world that they can do it on their own."

Tenney was and is perfectly happy with his present position, which frequently entails saddling Phipps horses for major stakes if McGaughey is out of town.

"There's been opportunities that have come along," Tenney said. "But I'm very, very happy with this job and always have been. These are very well-bred horses, and some of them turn out to be real good horses. I always liked the integrity side, no games. If a horse needs time off, he gets time off. You get to do the right thing by the horse. It's made for a pretty relaxed atmosphere, except for the pressure we put on ourselves and a little more. We place the bar pretty high."

McGaughey knows no other way. "I expect to do well," he said. "I can't stand to run a horse I know can't win, and I work as hard as I can. I understand the ups and downs of the game, but I expect, with the horses that I have, to do good. Buzzy is the kind of guy I can feel comfortable with."

Tenney's great aunt and uncle had Thoroughbreds on a farm outside Lexington, but that was the extent of his horse background. He graduated from the University of Mississippi with a business degree and absolutely no idea what he wanted to do next. "I went to work for my dad," he said. "He had a leasing business of automobiles and heavy equipment."

Tenney started working in collections and didn't particularly enjoy it. He switched to sales and still wasn't content. And then he decided to seek advice from a friend, a golf buddy named Seth Hancock, in September of 1977. "I really knew his sister, Dell, through my sister, Bitsy," Tenney said. "But I went out to Seth at Claiborne with my tie and coat on and told him I wasn't particularly thrilled with what I was doing. I was twenty-six, and I dreaded Mondays. I knew that wasn't the right way to live."

Hancock sent Tenney to see two people at Keeneland: Bill Evans, the director of sales, and Bill Greely, a vice president. Tenney, however, returned to Claiborne. "I told Seth they were very nice to me, but why don't I come back here and learn the business from the bottom up," Tenney said. "He said you work thirteen days for one day off. I said that was fine with me. I wanted to give it a try. I didn't want to go through life not knowing if I ever would have wanted to do it. I said, 'Fine. I don't care what the money is.' "

Tenney had a caveat. He told Hancock he could start the following Monday, after he saw Ole Miss battle Notre Dame in football on that Saturday. Hancock looked at Tenney kind of funny, but said okay. "Notre Dame killed them," Tenney confessed.

Two days later Tenney began a new career. He eventually landed with Steve Penrod, who trained Claiborne's Midwest division and wintered his horses at Aiken, South Carolina. "I went to Aiken with him one winter," Tenney said. "That was the end of farm life for me."

Tenney wanted to be closer to the racetrack, and he received an opportunity to do just that when McGaughey landed the Phipps' job and his assistant, Phil Hauswald, decided to open his own stable, inheriting several of McGaughey's former horses.

McGaughey and Tenney discussed the position over dinner at Mim's Steakhouse (now Pat's Steakhouse) in Louisville. "I agreed right there to go with him," Tenney said.

Together they framed a program to fit the Phipps horses. "I think one of the things Shug believes in most, as well as myself, is to put in a real good foundation, a bottom, in a horse," Tenney said. "Once they start breezing, they're still not asked for a lot of speed. Our horses are trained to relax early in their races and finish up. I think they do better being trained that way."

That does not preclude them from raising and racing a speed horse. "Inside Information [the 1995 champion older mare] had a lot of natural speed," Tenney said. "She'd run on the lead, but she'd relax on the lead. You get them relaxed right from the start. We concentrate a lot on the mental part."

Hancock remembers a recent phone conversation he had with an English bloodstock agent: "We were talking about Shug, and he said, 'He has the gypsy touch. It's a touch and a feel that he has.' I've talked to Dr. [Larry] Bramlage about Shug. Shug'll sit down and he'll see something in horses that other people won't. One thing is patience. He's got tremendous patience. Another thing about Shug is he might run a horse two or three times and then pick out some grade III stakes six months down the road. He'll point a horse to that day, and he'll run well that day."

McGaughey puts a lot of thought into what he's doing. "I try to bring a horse along in a way that he wants to," the trainer said. "I try to learn about him. Whether or not this is going to be a horse who's going to run as a two-year-old. Allow them to go up the ladder. I don't throw them to the dogs too early."

McGaughey likes to give his horses time and personal attention. He will employ six or seven exercise riders, while another stable might have three or four. McGaughey horses tour the backside as part of their daily routine. They don't just go from the barn to the track and back. McGaughey lets them stand on the racetrack before they exercise and gaze at their surroundings. He wants them to like their jobs. "I want the horse to have a good experience out there, where they think the racetrack is a good place to be," McGaughey said.

"I like a rider to be on the horse forty to forty-five minutes if he can," he said. "I come back in the afternoons and watch them walk and graze, monitor how they're eating and watch them. This is not a business to me."

To owners, of course, it is. The Phippses, however, also treat their horses as athletes and racing as a sport, giving McGaughey a luxury few trainers have: time. "If I have a two-year-old who turns an ankle, I can stop with him," McGaughey said. "It's a pleasure working with them [the Phippses] because they understand the game, and they want to do well."

And they trust their trainer to do that for them. "Dinny told me when we met the first time, 'The last

thing I hope is that anybody ever says we're hard to train for,' " McGaughey said. "And I've been here fifteen years, and only one time did Dinny ever question anything I did, and that was after the fact, when I decided to run Personal Ensign in the Beldame when she was a three-year-old instead of taking her to Kentucky and running her in the Spinster," related McGaughey. "He told me the Monday afterwards, 'I thought you were making a mistake, but you weren't, because she won.' There has never been anything by either one of them about doing anything wrong. They say, 'You run it and just keep us informed. It's your ballgame.' "

McGaughey stepped up to the plate in November of 1985.

# CHAPTER 5

## *At The Start*

McGaughey had barely settled into his role as private trainer of a forty-horse stable before he produced dramatic results. At the 1986 Gulfstream Park meet, which ran from early January through early March, he made quite a first impression. All he did was post fifteen victories, three seconds, and two thirds in twenty-nine starts. "We ended up having a big meeting at Gulfstream," McGaughey acknowledged. Only Woody Stephens had more wins with eighteen.

One of the unraced horses in the Phipps barn at Gulfstream was a three-year-old colt by Private Account out of Grecian Banner named Personal Flag. He would not make his debut until the subsequent Hialeah meet that spring. Although he finished fourth in his first start, he showed some promise and went on to win his next three starts before finishing fourth in the Belmont Stakes.

Later he added placings in the Dwyer Stakes, the Haskell Invitational, and the Travers Stakes. Racing against older horses, he also placed third in the Woodward Stakes behind Precisionist, champion sprinter in 1985, and eventual 1986 Horse of the Year Lady's Secret.

His full sister, Personal Ensign, was one of the two-year-olds shipped from Ocala to Keeneland in the spring of 1986. She started training at the pastoral Lexington track in April. She was a big, gangly dark bay with a white snip splitting her nostrils and another small white mark at the top of her head.

"I remember when she shipped in," her groom, Terry Cooney, said. "She didn't have a name then. She was the Grecian Banner filly. When they ship in, their halters are wrapped in strips of flannel. I was taking them all off. She wouldn't let me touch her. Wouldn't have anything to do with me."

It took Cooney several weeks to figure out Personal Ensign's quirks.

Depending on one's perspective, Personal Ensign was either ornery or strong-willed, stubborn or independent.

"You were not going to pet her," Lena Eriksson, one of Personal Ensign's exercise riders, said. "Cadillacing (another Phipps filly and future stakes winner born the same year), she wanted you to hug her and kiss her. They all have their personalities. They're all different."

Personal Ensign's first exercise rider, Jean Dolan, was impressed immediately. "She kept telling me that this filly can really run," McGaughey said. "She [Personal Ensign] hadn't shown me a whole lot. I was skeptical. She'd go a half [mile] in :50 or :51. Hell, anybody can do that. But she [Jean Dolan] kept telling me, 'This filly is something else.' "

Personal Ensign might have made her career debut in the summer of 1986 had she not developed a skin disease that took some time to clear up. Nevertheless, she shipped with the Phipps stable to the Oklahoma training track at Saratoga. And that was where McGaughey upgraded his opinion of his filly. "Oklahoma was a different track than it is now," he said. "It was about two seconds slower at least. And she worked a half in :49 here one morning."

McGaughey struggled to quell his enthusiasm. "Every year you're really basically looking to get a good horse out of the crop of two-year-olds you're getting," he said. "I maybe get more excited running a first time two-year-old I think can run than anything else in the business."

And this was his first crop of two-year-olds with the Phippses.

McGaughey had already settled on a rider for Personal Ensign: Randy Romero, the gutsy rider who emerged from the bush tracks in Louisiana to become one of the world's leading riders despite a freakish accident that nearly took his life at Oaklawn Park in 1983. While he was sitting in the sweatbox in the jockey's room covered with rubbing alcohol, a lightbulb exploded, igniting the alcohol. Romero suffered second- and third-degree burns over sixty percent of his body. Doctors gave him a forty percent chance to survive. He was back riding in fifteen weeks.

"I'm a survivor," he said. "I wouldn't let myself go down."

Romero's resiliency is documented by the twenty-two other more conventional accidents, twenty-one operations, and sixteen fractures he endured and recovered from during his riding career, which ended in July of 1999 at the age of forty-three. Now a jockey agent for Marlon St. Julien, who is also from Louisiana, Romero won 4,294 races and more than $75 million in his career.

From 1986 through 1990, Romero rode two of the most brilliant fillies ever to grace the racetrack, Personal Ensign and Go for Wand. Between them they had twenty-three wins and two seconds in twenty-five starts, not including Go for Wand's tragic accident in her final race in the 1990 Breeders' Cup Distaff.

"I can look back and see how fortunate I was to ride those two fillies," Romero said in 2001. "They were not just good fillies; they were champions. There's no geniuses in this game. You just do the best you can do. I was a hard worker and dedicated. Dedication brings you a lot. I tried not messing up. I wasn't better than anybody else. I was a lucky guy. It came down to timing."

Romero's was exquisite.

In 1985, while running horses at Churchill Downs, McGaughey and trainer Bill Mott were living in nearby townhouses in the same complex in Louisville. They were having dinner together with Romero, who was riding horses for both trainers. "We were all over in Bill's house eating dinner," McGaughey said. "We kind of walked out together.

"Randy said, 'I'm thinking about going to New York in the spring. Will you help me when I go up there?' "

"I said, 'Yeah, I'll help you.' "

McGaughey kept his word.

He gave Romero a leg up not only on Personal Ensign but also on Ogden Phipps' Polish Navy, destined to win his first four starts, including the grade I Cowdin and Champagne stakes in the fall of 1986.

On September 28, 1986, Personal Ensign stepped onto the mile and a half Belmont Park racetrack for her first start, a seven-furlong maiden race that would be contested on a muddy track. Talk of her ability preceded her debut. She went off at 9-10 in a field of seven. She seemed remarkably composed. "She went over to the paddock like John Henry," Buzz Tenney said.

Maybe she was too relaxed. When the starting gate opened, Personal Ensign hesitated. "She didn't break good," McGaughey recalled. Then again, McGaughey noted that Personal Ensign would seldom break well in subsequent races.

Romero did not panic on his first-time starter. "She was real late," he said. "She broke real bad. I just rode it the way the race came up. I let her get settled and she started running. The good ones overcome a lot."

But not as quickly as she did. Personal Ensign

circled the entire field with stunning ease, rallying from last in the field of seven to first before half a mile. And then she simply drew away, winning by twelve and three-quarter lengths in 1:22 4/5.

"You don't see horses do that very often," Romero said. "That was awesome. I never hit her with the stick. I think Shug knew she was good, but I didn't know if he thought she was that good. After I won on her, I said to him 'She's better than the colt (Polish Navy).' He said, 'You're kidding me.' I said, 'She is a freak.' I never rode anything like her. She is the real deal."

McGaughey confessed to being a bit startled by Personal Ensign's debut. "When you take one over there and you think they can run, and then they show you maybe they can *really* run, then it's a pretty exciting feeling," McGaughey said. "She exceeded our expectations, so we were a little bit in awe of what we saw. I didn't know she was that good."

He must have suspected, for he had nominated Personal Ensign for the grade I Frizette Stakes the day before her first race. "I wasn't impressed with what I saw in the other two-year-old fillies, so I said, 'Let me take a shot and nominate her,' " McGaughey said.

Coincidentally, the grade I Matron Stakes for two-year-old fillies was the same day as Personal Ensign's debut at the same distance of seven furlongs. Undefeated Tappiano upped her record to three for three, but took 1:23 2/5 to do so, three-fifths of a second slower than Personal Ensign's winning time in her first start.

Moving up a two-year-old from a maiden race to a grade I stakes was anything but the cautious route McGaughey usually takes with his horses. But Personal Ensign had shown him enough to take that risk. "When I reach out, I know what I'm reaching out with," he said.

Only five two-year-old fillies entered the thirty-ninth running of the $274,000 Frizette Stakes at one mile on Columbus Day, October 13 of 1986. Two of the quintet, Tappiano and Sea Basque, scratched when it rained earlier that day, but the Frizette was contested on a fast track by Personal Ensign, who would go off the 3-10 favorite, Tappiano's stablemate, Collins, and Flying Katuna.

Collins had won her debut, finished third to Sacahuista in the Schuylerville Stakes, second to her in the Adirondack, and fourth behind Delicate Vine, Sacahuista, and Ruling Angel in the Arlington-

Washington Lassie Stakes. Flying Katuna had broken her maiden the previous month at Belmont and was stakes-placed at Philadelphia.

Collins and Personal Ensign put on quite a show as the Frizette turned into a one-mile battle of will. Flying Katuna would never get involved.

Breaking from the outside three post under George Martens, Collins quickly spurted to a two and a half-length lead. Personal Ensign broke third, but quickly cut into Collins' lead, settling just behind her, glued to the outside of her flank. After half a mile, Collins' lead had narrowed to a head. Midway into Belmont Park's sweeping turn, Personal Ensign got within a head of the lead. Martens hit Collins once right-handed and then switched his stick to his left hand. Personal Ensign pushed a nose in front just before the eighth pole, but Collins refused to give in.

Martens hit Collins twelve times left-handed, while Romero used his stick eleven times right-handed as Personal Ensign maintained her minute advantage, winning by a head in 1:36 3/5 for the mile.

"She really had to run," Romero said.

And that might have been the key to her entire

career. "When Randy had to ask her to run a little bit that day, she learned about running, because she had never been asked to run," McGaughey said. "She didn't get anything from her maiden race. She came out of the Frizette a different horse. She knew what was going on. It was a wake-up call. Collins had a little more experience than she had. She was a little green that day."

But not afterward. "She showed me something right after the Frizette that I had never seen in a horse I've had," McGaughey said. "She'd go a minute like it was nothing. I've worked other horses faster, but it was the ease that she was doing it in. She was working with a 130- to 135-pound exercise rider. I never saw a horse change that quick."

Thirteen days after the Frizette, there was another change.

## Disaster

Personal Ensign was headed for the Breeders' Cup Juvenile Fillies at Santa Anita on November 1. A victory there would guarantee her the two-year-old filly championship. On a cold Sunday morning, the day before she was scheduled to fly to California, McGaughey supervised Personal Ensign's five-furlong breeze under exercise rider Jean Dolan.

"I remember like it was yesterday," assistant trainer Buzz Tenney said nearly fifteen years later. "It was raining. They decided not to have a harrowing break. I said, 'Shug, do you want to get this filly in early?' He said 'No.' "

There was quite a little crowd watching Personal Ensign's final work before leaving for the Breeders' Cup. Ogden Phipps was there, along with McGaughey's friend Rogers Beasley, the director of sales at Keeneland.

"She went in a minute and galloped out in :12," McGaughey recalled. The group sat and watched the filly cool out for approximately twenty-five minutes. By then, the cold was getting to Phipps, who decided to leave. McGaughey suggested that the others go to his office to warm up.

While the group headed indoors, Tenney went down to Personal Ensign's stall. Personal Ensign was standing quietly in her stall with the hotwalker, but to Tenney's surprise, the filly couldn't walk out of it. He put a blanket back on her and tried to give her more water, but she didn't want it. Surprise turned quickly to concern. Telling the hotwalker to keep Personal Ensign in the stall, Tenney rushed down to the barn office to get McGaughey. It seemed impossible that something could be wrong with the filly he thought had cooled out well.

McGaughey was shocked, too. He and Phipps had watched her cool out the whole time and had seen no signs that anything was amiss. Now she was lame and couldn't walk. McGaughey immediately sent for the vet.

Dr. Jim Hunt took X-rays that revealed Personal Ensign had fractured her left rear pastern, the bone just above her ankle. Presumably, she broke it during her breeze, though she gave no indication of discomfort immediately afterward, likely due to endorphins that kicked in and masked the initial pain. But now the endorphins had worn off, Personal Ensign was hurting, and McGaughey had some tough calls to make.

The trainer had the unpleasant duty of making the arrangements for an operation and informing Phipps and his son of the bad news.

"Shug handles these things better than he handles a skin disease or cracked heels, things you can avoid," Tenney said. "Fracture? That's just an ugly part of the game. That's going to happen."

McGaughey was convinced that his star filly's career was over. But he was encouraged when he realized the fracture could be fixed and that her life was not in danger.

Dinny Phipps remembers McGaughey's phone call. "It's got to be the toughest call for a trainer to make," he said. "But it's not something he created or did. It happens. He takes it personally. If you didn't care, it wouldn't affect you personally."

Dr. Larry Bramlage, one of the most esteemed veterinarians in the country, was in O'Hare Airport in Chicago, on his way from New York to California, when his secretary called and told him about Personal Ensign. He called McGaughey's barn and spoke with Tenney. Bramlage then went on to California as planned to take care of an injured horse, and took the red-eye back to New York so he could operate on Personal Ensign the next morning at Dr. William Reed's clinic across the street from Belmont Park.

Bramlage looked at Personal Ensign's X-rays and liked what he saw. "She had an unusual fracture," he said. "Most horses, when they break the long pastern bone, they fracture it from front to back. She fractured it from side to side."

The difference? It was easier to fix.

Bramlage inserted five stainless-steel implementation screws to hold the bone together. "When we put the fracture back together, it went together very nicely, right back to where it came from," he said. "We wanted to make the two joints as secure as we could. When we tightened the screws, she recovered quickly. She showed class and got up very well. She wore the cast for a couple of weeks and then we took it off."

In the interim Reed told McGaughey, "I think she'll be all right."

"What do you mean, she'll be all right?" the trainer asked.

"I think she'll race again," was the reply.

McGaughey wasn't convinced, so he called Bramlage.

"I'm confident she'll be able to be a broodmare and there's some chance that she might race," Bramlage told the skeptical trainer.

"You mean go back and race like the way she was racing?"

"We'll have to wait and see."

And still McGaughey had his doubts. "Well, it was hard to believe," he said later.

Ironically, Personal Ensign's misstep provided Bramlage with a springboard to international acclaim. In the years since, he has emerged as a leading equine veterinary surgeon, operating on legions of famous racehorses and prized breeding stock. "I was a young professional at the time," he said. "She did a lot for my credibility. She is my favorite horse without a doubt."

Bramlage has gone on to become a veterinary commentator on national television during major race coverage. He is a partner in the Rood and Riddle Equine Hospital in Lexington, Kentucky, and the consulting surgeon for Lloyd's of London Insurance Company. He received The Jockey Club Gold Medal for Contributions to Thoroughbred Racing in 1994.

Asked the prognosis for a horse to return to racing today with the same fracture Personal Ensign suffered, he said, "Fifty percent. The prognosis back then was maybe twenty-five percent."

But even if she could return to race, how could she possibly realize the immense potential she had displayed in her first two starts?

Seth Hancock of Claiborne Farm likened it to a running back having total reconstructive surgery on a knee and then leading the National Football League in rushing. Things like that just don't happen.

Other questions lingered. How would people react if she returned to racing and hurt herself worse or even died on the track?

At the time, there seemed to be little upside to the possibility of a return.

# CHAPTER 7

## *Return?*

P ersonal Ensign spent the winter of 1986-87 in New York in her stall and under the watchful eyes of Shug McGaughey, Dr. Larry Bramlage, and Dr. Jim Hunt. Having been stallbound for ninety days, she began her physical rehabilitation in early February with walking, and she was led by hand for forty-five days. She then progressed to walking under tack in mid-April.

"She did that very well," Bramlage said. "Shug was pretty conservative with her. As she healed and the bone showed increased strength, it progressed as if you had written it out like a script."

Not quite. McGaughey began training her later that spring, and he was not happy with her progress. "She was training along and training along, and she had a lot of antibiotics," McGaughey said. "And I remember, it was around the first of July, and Mr. Phipps said to me:

"Shug, she looks terrible."

"I agree. She looks awful. I don't know why."

McGaughey was stumped. "She didn't physically look good," he said, explaining that her coat was dull and she had lost weight, not to mention conditioning.

Friends would stop by the barn to see her and were surprised by her appearance. Personal Ensign seemed to be doing fine otherwise, so McGaughey decided to pick up her training to see whether that would help. He shipped her to Saratoga to work on the Oklahoma training track, where she had been prepared as a two-year-old.

The Spa reinvigorated Personal Ensign. With each two-minute gallop and slow breeze, she improved, even as McGaughey worried about her injured leg. "I tried to take all the precautions," he said. "Is there something going on back there that I'm not seeing? I was concerned every time I did something with her."

The day before her final work, he ordered X-rays. But the X-rays were perfect.

The next morning McGaughey knew she had turned the corner. In her final move Personal Ensign impressed one of McGaughey's exercise riders, an Englishman named Bob Witham, who rode another of the trainer's horses that morning.

"How did your horse go?" McGaughey asked Witham.

"Mine went fine," replied the rider. "I don't know who the one next to me is, but she's something extra."

McGaughey said, "Well, she can really run."

McGaughey searched for the right spot for his filly. He wanted to put her in an allowance race for non-winners of two races other than maiden or claiming. Personal Ensign fit the conditions because she only had her maiden win and a stakes win. But the race didn't fill, so he entered her in a "three other than."

On September 6, 1987, eleven months after winning the Frizette, Personal Ensign returned to the races in a seven-furlong allowance against five other fillies and mares. Her jockey was Jerry Bailey. Randy Romero was scheduled to ride Dance of Life in the Arlington Million.

McGaughey told Romero to go to Chicago to ride in the Million. "This is only an allowance race. Win, lose, or draw, you've got her back," the trainer told the jockey.

Ironically, Romero's horse was scratched in the Million. Under Bailey, Personal Ensign was sent off the

7-10 favorite in her return. She broke fifth, settled in fourth after a quarter mile, and won easily by three and three-quarter lengths, getting seven furlongs in 1:23 1/5.

Like so many others, Romero marveled at the job McGaughey had done bringing her back. "He's patient and very smart," Romero said. "Shug is a perfectionist. It's a good thing, but he's hard on himself. He really is."

Romero was back in New York for Personal Ensign's next start, a $33,000 allowance race, but McGaughey was not. He was in North Carolina on an annual golf trip he wished he had never planned. He called Belmont Park from a pay phone at the golf course. "I was a nervous wreck," he said. "I was always nervous when she raced."

But McGaughey kept the pressure of maintaining her undefeated career well hidden. While on his trip, he listened by phone to the call of her seven and three-quarter-length romp. She had run a mile in 1:36 1/5, with the final quarter in a quick :24 3/5. She was back. She had even broken better, getting away second in the field of five.

She was ready for a step up. Personal Ensign had

proven she could compete again and win races, but could she do so at the highest level? The grade II Rare Perfume Stakes at Belmont Park on October 10 would provide an answer.

The bettors thought she was up to the task, sending her off at 4-5 in the mile event. She was facing a solid field of nine, including One From Heaven, who had won four stakes and finished third in the Queen's Plate in Canada that year; Chic Shirine, who had won the grade I Ashland; Mar Mar, who had captured the Bonnie Miss at Gulfstream Park; Firey Challenge, who had taken the Prioress Stakes at Belmont; Key Bid, who had won two allowances at Saratoga and had placed in seven stakes that season; and Valid Line, who had captured stakes at Meadowlands and Monmouth Park.

Leaving from the two post, Personal Ensign broke eighth but quickly rushed up into a stalking position in fourth, inside of Firey Challenge, as Valid Line and Mar Mar dueled on the lead through a quick quarter in :22 3/5. Heading to the half, Romero shot Personal Ensign up three wide and she took over readily, getting the half-mile in :45 4/5. Firey Challenge tried following her move but could not sustain it as Personal

Independent and willful, Personal Ensign simply refused to be beaten. She accrued thirteen wins in thirteen starts to become the first major American Thoroughbred since Colin eighty years earlier to retire undefeated.

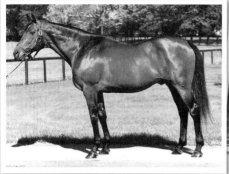

Ogden Phipps' homebred Private
Account (above), sire of Personal
Ensign, was a solid stakes winner and
sire. Out of Phipps' champion mare
Numbered Account, Private Account
is by Horse of the Year Damascus
(above right).

Argentinian import Dorine (right) and
champion two-year-old Hoist the Flag
(below right) came together to produce Grecian Banner (pictured below
with her most famous offspring).

The Phipps family has been in horse racing for more than eight decades, starting with Gladys Livingston Mills Phipps (right), who owned Wheatley Stable with her brother. Her son, Ogden (above right with his grandson Ogden II), has raced numerous stakes winners as has his son, Ogden Mills (Dinny) Phipps (above, on right with trainer Shug McGaughey).

Trainer Shug McGaughey (below) and his friend and assistant Buzz Tenney (left) were integral to Personal Ensign's success, as were her regular jockey Randy Romero (below left) and groom Terry Cooney (bottom, with her famous charge).

Personal Ensign showed star quality with her victory in the Frizette (below). But her burgeoning career was considered over after she suffered a broken left hind pastern in a subsequent work. Equine surgeon Larry Bramlage (above) repaired the break by inserting five screws in her leg (right).

Personal Ensign, shown above left
with exercise rider Lena Eriksson,
made a successful return to the track
almost a year after her accident.
She captured two allowance events
against older mares, then romped
home in the Rare Perfume
(above right). In her final start
at three, she faced older mares
again to capture the Beldame.

In 1988 Personal Ensign made the most of a full season. She warmed up with a victory in the Shuvee (above right), then devastated her rivals by seven in the Hempstead (above left). McGaughey led his star to a familiar spot — the winner's circle — after the Hempstead.

Traveling outside New York
for the first time, Personal
Ensign wowed New Jersey
fans in the Molly Pitcher
(opposite, top). She showed
her feisty side at Saratoga as
she readied for her next test
in the Whitney Handicap.
Neither the boys nor the slop
could stop her, though, as she
splashed to victory (right).

Foreshadowing a future race, Personal Ensign faced off against 1988 Kentucky Derby winner Winning Colors in the Maskette (above and below) and held her safe. In her last start before the Breeders' Cup, Personal Ensign easily captured her second Beldame (right).

Personal Ensign was all business for the Breeders' Cup Distaff, from the post parade (right) to the homestretch, where she gamely rallied on a surface she hated, just catching Winning Colors and Goodbye Halo in a heart-pounding finish to win by a nose.

After Personal Ensign's thrilling Distaff victory, Randy Romero let the world know she was "No. 1." Personal Ensign retired undefeated and was named champion older mare for 1988.

Personal Ensign returned to her birthplace, Claiborne Farm in Kentucky, to begin a new phase as a broodmare.

Personal Ensign got off to an auspicious start as a brood-mare. Her first foal, Miner's Mark, won the grade I Jockey Club Gold Cup (top). Three years later, she produced a chestnut filly (left) by Ogden Phipps' homebred champion Easy Goer. The filly, named My Flag, won the 1995 Breeders' Cup Juvenile Fillies (above), making Personal Ensign the first mare to win a Breeders' Cup race and produce a Breeders' Cup winner.

In 1997 Personal Ensign foaled a colt by Mr. Prospector (left). Named Traditionally, he became his dam's third grade I winner when he won the 2001 Oaklawn Handicap (above). Personal Ensign survived a difficult foaling in 1998. Two years later she produced Possibility, a filly by A.P. Indy (below).

At age seventeen in 2001, Personal Ensign still retains the spirited nature that made her a champion on the racetrack. She has continued to receive accolades, including Hall of Fame induction in 1993 and Broodmare of the Year honors in 1996.

BROODMARE AWARD
OF 1996
KENTUCKY THOROUGHBRED OWNERS AND BREEDERS
PERSONAL ENSIGN
(1984)
PRIVATE ACCOUNT        GRECIAN BANNER
(SIRE)                          (DAM)
OGDEN PHIPPS
(OWNER)

Ensign shook free from the entire field. She roared to the top of the stretch in complete control, getting six furlongs in 1:10 2/5. Heading to the eighth pole, Romero showed her the whip once right-handed. Passing the eighth pole, he glanced back quickly over his right shoulder. There was nobody there.

As track announcer John Imbriale called, "She's going to remain unbeaten," Personal Ensign eased to the wire four and three-quarter lengths ahead of One From Heaven, completing the mile in 1:36 3/5. Key Bid was well back in third.

"This was her best effort yet," McGaughey told Russ Harris, the noted handicapper of the *New York Daily News* who covered the race for *The Blood-Horse*. "This was the best field she's run against, and to beat a nice group of fillies that way is pretty encouraging."

Romero came to his own conclusion: "She got better with age. The guy who did the operation did an excellent job. He was a genius. She was like a genius herself. I didn't worry about pace, being inside or outside, mud or dirt. Nothing bothered her."

McGaughey weighed two options for her next start: remain at Belmont Park for the grade I Beldame Stakes against older fillies and mares just eight days later or wait until October 31 and ship to Keeneland for the grade I Spinster Stakes, also against older fillies and mares.

She stayed in New York. "Just because it was home and we didn't have to ship," McGaughey said.

Personal Ensign had beaten older mares twice in allowance company, but the Beldame was a major stakes at a mile and a quarter. And it marked an enormous competitive leap for the daughter of Private Account.

For the lone time in her career, she would not go off the favorite, although it took a five-horse entry to deny her that role. The entry went off .90-to-1, Personal Ensign at 1.30-to-1 in the field of ten.

The entry of common ownership combined two horses trained by Jan Nerud, the son of Hall of Fame trainer John Nerud, and three trained by D. Wayne Lukas. Nerud saddled Coup de Fusil, who had won three grade I stakes in succession: the Ruffian (on a disqualification) and the John A. Morris and Delaware handicaps, and multiple stakes winner Funistrada. Lukas' trio were Fiesta Gal, winner of the Mother Goose and Coaching Club American Oaks; Without Feathers, winner of the Monmouth Oaks; and Clabber

Girl, who had finished second to Coup de Fusil in both the Ruffian and John A. Morris.

Breaking from the eight post, Personal Ensign got away quickly and settled in behind battling leaders Coup de Fusil on the rail and Without Feathers alongside. Past an incredibly slow first quarter of :25, Romero asked Personal Ensign to move, and she went after Without Feathers, who had managed to almost clear Coup de Fusil. Personal Ensign raced three-quarters of a length off Without Feathers and whittled away her lead to half a length, then a neck through a half-mile in :49 3/5. And, then, Personal Ensign took off and left her older rivals behind.

In a near replay of her move in the Rare Perfume, she opened a lead of three to four lengths coming out of the far turn. Unlike the Rare Perfume, however, Romero had to remind her to stay focused, tapping her nine times right-handed through the stretch as she cruised home a two and a quarter-length winner over Coup de Fusil in 2:04 2/5 for the mile and a quarter.

"I had no idea how she would run today, coming back eight days after the other race," McGaughey told *The Blood-Horse*'s Ernie Munick. "She has never run against this kind. I thought she would go a distance, but you don't know unless you try it."

Romero told Munick that Personal Ensign was the fastest filly he'd ever ridden: "If she gets in trouble, she is so fast she can get out of it."

She had found no trouble despite racing with five screws in one of her ankles. "That thing never did bother her," McGaughey said.

A victory in the Breeders' Cup Distaff at Hollywood Park would have clinched the three-year-old filly championship, but the Breeders' Cup was unusually late that year, November 21, more than a month after the Beldame.

McGaughey decided to bypass it, shipping her to Florida instead to prepare for her four-year-old campaign. Personal Ensign thus ended her three-year-old season with four wins in four starts and earned $302,640.

Personal Ensign did not win a championship. That honor went to the Lukas-trained Sacahuista, who had won the 1987 Cotillion and Ruffian handicaps, only to be disqualified in both. After the last disqualification, Lukas made a jockey change to a rider he knew was good with fillies: Randy Romero.

With Personal Ensign getting some rest and relaxation, Romero rode Sacahuista to a three-length win in the Spinster and a two and a quarter-length victory in the Distaff. Sacahuista was voted the three-year-old filly championship.

Despite Personal Ensign's losing the championship, McGaughey and the Phippses took comfort in the remarkable fact that their filly had returned to race at all.

"We had gotten her back. We had accomplished what we wanted to do," McGaughey said. "We said, 'Next year, we'll get a full campaign for her.'"

# CHAPTER 8

## *Better Than Ever*

P ersonal Ensign liked her independence. Her new exercise rider, Lena Eriksson, quickly got the hint.

Eriksson became Personal Ensign's exercise rider in December 1987. Jean Dolan, who had breezed the filly the morning she broke her pastern, left the stable after the horse was injured. Another rider, Liz Palmer, took a vacation and never came back.

A native of Sweden, Eriksson came to the United States in 1984 and began working for McGaughey that fall at Churchill Downs.

When she learned the stable needed an exercise rider in Florida the winter of 1987, she quickly volunteered. "Shug said, 'When do you want to start?' I said, 'Tomorrow if I can,' " she recalled.

When she began exercising Personal Ensign, Eriksson got the distinct impression that her filly knew just how good she was. "I think she knew she was special," Eriksson said. "I think good horses do. They like to train, but they're opinionated. They're more leaders than followers. They're professionals. A good horse will learn quickly, and they really like their job. Maybe it's because it's easier for them. The good horses, their mind is set a little different."

Despite Personal Ensign's superior attitude, Eriksson had no trouble with her. "She was a little independent. She didn't want you to mess with her, but she was not difficult to ride. She liked to have company, a pony named Levi or Whitey, both grays."

Eriksson worked Personal Ensign slowly most mornings. After workouts they would go for a long walk and Eriksson would let her filly graze. When they returned to the barn, Personal Ensign would have her bath and be turned over to a hotwalker for a half-hour. Sometimes Personal Ensign would be walked and grazed for a good hour. Then the hotwalker would hose down her legs, a standard procedure for all the horses, and the filly would be brought back to her stall. Afterward her groom, Terry Cooney, would put bandages on her as a precaution.

On race days Eriksson would ride Personal Ensign's pony alongside her in the post parade. "You don't get a very good view of the race because you're watching from the gate," she said. "You pray that nothing bad is going to happen."

When McGaughey shipped some horses to New York from Gulfstream Park for a week, Eriksson accompanied them. David Carroll, a native of Ireland who was already exercising several of the stable's top horses, was Personal Ensign's temp.

"I galloped her for one week, the longest week of my life," said Carroll, who worked for McGaughey from 1986 through 1990. Carroll then worked under Peter Vestal for two years before opening his own stable, which he races at Churchill Downs and Fair Grounds.

Every time Carroll got on Personal Ensign that week at Gulfstream Park, foreman Tony Reinstedler, also now training his own stable, would remind Carroll: "Don't mess her up. I don't want to be making that phone call to Shug."

Carroll had his hands full. "I was galloping Easy Goer and Seeking the Gold and Personal Flag, and I knew their idiosyncrasies," he said. "They were my horses, and I had a comfort level with them.

"I didn't want anything to happen to her while I was riding her. There was a little extra pressure."

Personal Ensign, knowing she had a stranger on her back, did not help. "She was very intelligent. She took advantage of that," Carroll recalled. "Lena rode the filly with a longer rein. I rode my horses with a shorter one, but I tried riding her with a longer one. She was strong. I have a picture at home of me pulling her up. My face is as red as a beet. 'Get me off of her!' "

When he wasn't riding her that week, Carroll kept his distance. "She took care of her territory," he said. "Nobody could get near her except Terry."

As Personal Ensign neared her return to racing fitness, McGaughey unsuccessfully sought an allowance race in New York for her four-year-old debut. Instead, he was forced to run her in the Shuvee Handicap for her first start after a seven-month hiatus.

If ever Personal Ensign would be vulnerable, the grade I Shuvee, at a mile and a sixteenth, on May 15, 1988, seemed like the spot. Personal Ensign was coming off a long layoff and going that distance for the first time, though she had raced ten furlongs previously. And, with a career high weight of 121, she was giving three pounds to Clabber Girl, who had just won the Top Flight Handicap, also a grade I.

Regardless, Personal Ensign went off the 7-10 favorite in the six-horse field. But there were anxious moments.

Personal Ensign broke last, but quickly rushed into third behind pace-setting Bishop's Delight, who ripped off a half in :45 3/5 to clear herself of the graded stakes-winning Mausie. Personal Ensign moved up boldly two-wide, but Clabber Girl was moving right with her three-wide and seemed to have more momentum coming out of the turn after three-quarters in a demanding 1:10. Bishop's Delight was exceedingly game along the rail, but Personal Ensign, racing in between horses, finally edged clear at the eighth-pole with Romero hitting her six times. Still, Personal Ensign had Clabber Girl breathing down her neck. "When Clabber Girl got as close as a half-length, I thought she had me," McGaughey said afterward.

Instead, with Romero using the whip six more times left-handed, Personal Ensign shook free of Clabber Girl to win by a length and three-quarters in 1:41 3/5. Bishop's Delight, a minor stakes winner, held on for third.

Personal Ensign was now seven for seven and ready for more.

Only four fillies and mares opposed her in the mile and an eighth grade I Hempstead Handicap on June 11. Carrying high weight of 123 pounds, she went off at 2-5. And she was breathtaking.

With the speedy Bishop's Delight back for another shot, Romero let Personal Ensign settle in third. When a duel between Bishop's Delight and Scorned Lass on the front end ensued inside of her, Personal Ensign became the beneficiary of a perfect trip.

When Romero asked his filly for run, she accelerated, taking the lead at the top of the stretch. At the eighth pole, with Romero sitting motionless, Personal Ensign opened up on the field. At the sixteenth pole she poured it on, winning by seven lengths in 1:47 3/5 off a final eighth in :12 flat. "I was just patient with her, and I knew that whenever I wanted to make my move she was ready," Romero told Bill Finley of *The Blood-Horse*. "We had straight dead aim on all of them."

There were story lines galore that weekend at

Belmont Park. In the three-year-old filly division, Kentucky Derby winner Winning Colors faltered badly behind runaway winner Risen Star in the Belmont Stakes, losing by forty-one and three-quarter lengths. The day before, Goodbye Halo, who at the time was the only filly to beat Winning Colors — they had split their two meetings — stated her case for the leadership of the division by winning the grade I Mother Goose Stakes, making her lifetime record seven wins in nine starts. Goodbye Halo, Winning Colors, and Personal Ensign would all meet in the Breeders' Cup Distaff later that year.

Then there were two family stories. One was Secretariat's son, Risen Star, winning the Belmont Stakes by fourteen and three-quarter lengths fifteen years after his famous father completed the Triple Crown by taking the Belmont by thirty-one lengths in a world record 2:24 for the mile and a half.

Personal Ensign had her own family tale. The day after the Hempstead, her full brother, Personal Flag, captured the Nassau County Handicap, but in a starkly different manner. Personal Flag was all out to beat Cryptoclearance by three-quarters of a length.

Personal Ensign was ready for bigger targets. A championship. A Horse of the Year title. But questions persisted. "We got some knocks, 'Well, she only wins at Belmont Park,' " McGaughey said.

So he declined to start brother and sister in the same stakes race, the Suburban Handicap, leaving Personal Flag at Belmont Park and taking Personal Ensign across the river to New Jersey to compete in the Molly Pitcher Handicap the same afternoon at Monmouth Park. Personal Ensign's record was a perfect eight for eight, but her critics had a point. All eight races were at Belmont Park. What would happen on the road?

# CHAPTER 9

## *Celebration*

O gden Phipps had more to celebrate than most Americans on the July Fourth weekend of 1988. On Friday, July 2, his Seeking the Gold won the grade I Dwyer Stakes at Belmont Park. On July 4, Personal Flag won the grade I Suburban Handicap at Belmont over the heavily favored Bet Twice.

Later that afternoon Phipps boarded a helicopter and flew to Monmouth Park to watch Personal Flag's younger sister put her eight-for-eight record on the line in the grade II Molly Pitcher Handicap. Carrying 125 pounds, six to fourteen pounds more than her four rivals, she was making her first start away from Belmont Park.

Sent off at 2-5 in the mile and a sixteenth stakes, Personal Ensign broke last in the field of five and then was three wide on the first turn. Grecian Flight, making her third stakes start in less than three weeks, cruised loose on the lead through a quarter in :24 and a half-mile in :47 2/5. She was still three lengths ahead of Personal Ensign, who had taken over second.

Personal Ensign made her customary move on the turn and quickly reached even terms with Grecian Flight by the head of the stretch. In an instant it was over. Personal Ensign powered away to win by eight lengths in 1:41 4/5, just three-fifths of a second off the stakes record shared by Ambassador of Luck and Lady's Secret. "Once she got near the far turn, I just let out a notch on the rein, and she took off," Romero said.

McGaughey looked over the remaining stakes in the summer and did not see many options for his undefeated filly. She had beaten the best of her division. So he pointed her north for a date with colts in the grade I Whitney Handicap at Saratoga. "It's a calculated risk, but we have a lot of confidence in her," McGaughey told Tim Wilkin of the *Albany Times Union*. "I think we have the horse to beat."

Only two would even try: Gulch and King's Swan, two horses of vastly different backgrounds and ages.

Gulch, a four-year-old son of Mr. Prospector, had been brilliant early in his career, winning his first five races. After taking his debut by seven and three-quarter lengths, he ripped off victories in the grade III Tremont, grade II Saratoga Special, and a pair of grade I stakes, the Hopeful and Futurity. Capote ended Gulch's winning streak, defeating him in both the grade I Norfolk Stakes and the Breeders' Cup Juvenile. At three Gulch won the Bay Shore, Wood Memorial, and Metropolitan Handicap, beating none other than King's Swan by a neck. After losing the final seven starts of his three-year-old season, Gulch switched barns from LeRoy Jolley to D. Wayne Lukas.

At four Gulch won an allowance race and the Potrero Grande Handicap at Santa Anita before finishing third in the grade I Oaklawn Handicap to Lost Code. He then won back-to-back grade I stakes, the Carter and his second Metropolitan, before finishing second to Cutlass Reality in the grade I Californian. In his final start before the 1988 Whitney, Gulch was second by three-quarters of a length as the odds-on favorite in the grade II Tom Fool Stakes at Belmont Park to King's Swan, who, at the age of eight, was twice Gulch's age.

While Gulch had sparkled from the minute he stepped onto the track as a two-year-old, King's Swan had not. The son of King's Bishop lost both his starts at two and his first one at three before taking a $50,000 maiden claimer at Aqueduct on January 30, 1983, more than a year before Personal Ensign was foaled.

King's Swan was a solid racehorse through his five-year-old season, winning eleven of forty-four starts and $212,350. In 1985 trainer Dick Dutrow claimed him for $80,000, and, under his tutelage, King's Swan kicked it up a notch, earning the nickname "King of Aqueduct" for his many stakes victories there. The following year, the six-year-old King's Swan won eight of fifteen starts and $451,207. One of his losses was in the Whitney Handicap, when he finished fifth by ten lengths to Lady's Secret. At seven, King's Swan had three wins, six seconds, and two thirds in twelve starts for earnings of $477,218. At the age of eight in 1988, on the way to his best year in earnings, $539,681, King's Swan took another shot at a filly in the Whitney Handicap in his eighty-second start.

Gulch was the Whitney highweight at 124, giving King's Swan one pound and Personal Ensign seven. Jose Santos rode Gulch, who went off at 9-5. King's Swan was 2-1 under Angel Cordero Jr., and Personal Ensign and Romero were 4-5.

When a severe early afternoon thunderstorm pelted Saratoga racecourse for twenty minutes, turning the track into slop, McGaughey almost scratched Personal Ensign. Her absence would have reduced the Whitney to a match race between two New York-based horses who had just raced against each other.

"We weren't going to run on an off track, and it rained before the first race," McGaughey said. "I went over to the barn as soon as it started raining. And I remember going over to the track and watching the third race. The water was just on top. It sounded like the horses weren't getting to the bottom — there wasn't that clickety-clack, clickety-clack sound. There was still some cushion, so we elected to run."

On a track labeled sloppy, Gulch, who would go on to win the Breeders' Cup Sprint and the sprint championship, seemed to have a decided edge, dictating the pace in a field of just three. Breaking from the two post, with King's Swan inside him, Gulch quickly angled over to the rail, nearly cutting off King's Swan, who settled into a stalking position in second. Romero kept Personal Ensign in third, two to three lengths behind Gulch through a half-mile in :47 2/5. Heading

into the far turn, King's Swan made another surge to draw within a length of the leader, but behind them, Personal Ensign accelerated with a sudden, dramatic rush, drawing even with Gulch midway on the turn.

She looked like she would sustain her momentum and take control of the race, but Gulch had plenty left, and they hooked up like champions do, shoulder to shoulder, head to head, and eye to eye.

The sun had poked free of the clouds and illuminated their battle: Gulch on the inside under a left-hand whip, Personal Ensign on the outside under Romero's right-handed insistence. Maybe one-hundred yards before the wire, Personal Ensign shook free of Gulch and was actually drawing away, winning the Whitney by a hard-earned length and a half in 1:47 4/5. The time was just four-fifths of a second slower than Tri Jet's stakes and track record.

"The filly was getting seven pounds; it's a lot," Santos said. "Gulch tried to come back, but he couldn't. He ran hard and he was tired at the end."

Personal Ensign was now ten for ten after a performance Bill Finley called "electric" in *The Blood-Horse*. Gulch's trainer, Lukas, called it "a great race and a great race for the sport." Dutrow said, "I would truly take my hat off to the filly. She's incredible."

Returning to a round of applause ringing the Saratoga winner's circle, Romero held his right index finger in the air. The gesture was more than symbolic, for her Whitney victory would propel Personal Ensign to the top spot in the weekly poll by Thoroughbred Racing Communications. If Horse of the Year balloting had been held that week, she would have won, mirroring Lady's Secret path to the title through the Whitney two years earlier.

"She's for real," Romero said. "A real champion."

Cordero believed. After the race, he told the *Albany Times Union*, "I thought she was the best thing I've seen since Ruffian. Now, I think she's better than Ruffian."

Twelve years have not altered Cordero's opinion. "In the late sixties and early seventies, we had great fillies," he said. "I think Personal Ensign was a much better filly than all of them. To me, she was one of the greatest fillies we ever had. And I never rode her. She was consistent. She broke down and she came back. She overcame a lot. To be a champion, you have to overcome a lot. You have to be able to overcome pressure."

And the pressure on Personal Ensign's connections was increasing exponentially. The Phippses had decided she had proved just about all she had needed to and announced that Personal Ensign would finish her career in the 1988 Breeders' Cup Distaff.

McGaughey told *The Blood-Horse*:

"It'll be odd when I lead her to the paddock for the last time. For the better part of two years, I've been coming to the barn every morning, and she's always been the main thing on my mind. I go to her stall and see how she is, if she's doing good. When I think of everything I've done with her every morning, there will be a void there. But I'm satisfied with everything we've done with her."

Turf writers had determined that if she finished her career undefeated, she would be America's first major undefeated horse since Colin went fifteen for fifteen in a two-year career that ended with his two-length victory in the Tidal Stakes at Sheepshead Bay Racetrack in New York, June 20, 1908.

Personal Ensign was chasing history. Soon she would be chasing the winner of the Kentucky Derby.

# PERSONAL ENSIGN

# CHAPTER 10

## *Chasing Colors*

On August 13, 1987, in Saratoga, Randy Romero climbed aboard a first-time starter owned by Eugene V. Klein, who also owned the National Football League's San Diego Chargers. The two-year-old roan filly Winning Colors, a daughter of Caro trained by D. Wayne Lukas, was bet down to 9-5 in her debut against ten rivals.

She broke on top, set serious fractions of :22 1/5 for a quarter and :45 3/5 for a half-mile, extended the lead to four lengths, and coasted home a two and a half-length winner, getting seven furlongs in 1:24 1/5.

She would use her natural speed throughout her career to sprint away from any horse that tried to run with her. Romero never rode her again. But he did ride against her twice.

The following spring Winning Colors made racing history. Following her smashing seven and a half-length victory over colts in the Santa Anita Derby, Winning Colors became just the third filly to win the Kentucky Derby. She grimly held off Forty Niner to win by a neck after leading all the way. That made Winning Colors six for seven lifetime; the lone blemish a second by a neck to Goodbye Halo in the grade I Las Virgenes, a loss she immediately avenged in the grade I Santa Anita Oaks.

In the Preakness Forty Niner pushed Winning Colors early and aggressively, but she held on gamely for third behind Risen Star and Brian's Time. That race may have taken a lot out of her. In the Belmont Stakes, Winning Colors stopped badly, finishing sixth by more than forty-one lengths to runaway winner Risen Star.

Lukas gave his filly a deserved rest and then asked her to return in the grade I Maskette on September 10 against older fillies and mares. One of her opponents was bringing a ten-race winning streak to the battle.

Only one other time in modern racing history had a filly with a ten-for-ten record met the Kentucky Derby winner in a race at Belmont Park. In 1975, Ruffian put her perfect record on the line in a match race against the Kentucky Derby winner, Foolish Pleasure. Tragedy ensued, and Ruffian lost her life.

In 1988, Personal Ensign put her perfect record on the line against the Kentucky Derby winner, Winning Colors. What followed was a tremendous race.

The one-mile Maskette, where Personal Ensign might have been more vulnerable to a top-quality speed horse such as Winning Colors, was not originally on McGaughey's fall schedule to get Personal Ensign to the Breeders' Cup Distaff. He had intended to run her in the Ruffian at a mile and an eighth.

"But we decided to go with the Maskette because it was weight for age, really not knowing Winning Colors was going to be there. But we made our decision. And when Winning Colors decided to go, that was the way it was going to be."

Still, the thought of Winning Colors running loose on the lead concerned McGaughey, so he decided to enter a rabbit — a front-runner that would ensure a quick pace. The filly he chose was Cadillacing, Easy Goer's older sister who had won the grade I Ballerina Stakes at Saratoga.

Only three other fillies entered the Maskette: Sham Say, Thirty Zip, and Fara's Team, who was scratched early.

McGaughey then changed his mind and scratched Cadillacing late. "It was the third race, and Cordero was going to ride the rabbit, and he came to me and said that Lukas was livid that he was going to ride the rabbit, and this and that," McGaughey said. "And I said, 'Okay, we'll just scratch the rabbit.' Then during the race, Winning Colors is six in front going down the backside, and I'm going, 'What an idiot I am.' I don't know if we'll be able to beat her."

Though Personal Ensign carried 123 pounds, five more than Winning Colors, she was the 3-10 favorite. Winning Colors was second choice at 2-1.

It took all of two seconds for Winning Colors to spring from the outside post to the lead under Gary Stevens, who had ridden the filly in every start except her first. Stevens immediately sensed that this was not the same filly who folded so badly in the Belmont Stakes. "I could tell her stride was back," Stevens said. "She felt the way she did in the Derby."

And she raced just as she had in the Derby: alone on the lead. But the fractions she laid down were grueling. After scooting the first quarter in :22 4/5, she sizzled a second quarter in an even faster :22 2/5 to hit the half in :45 1/5, five lengths in front of Sham Say in second.

Personal Ensign had broken last and then settled in

third behind Winning Colors and Sham Say. After a half-mile Personal Ensign was at least six lengths behind the leader.

But Personal Ensign suddenly accelerated. By running her own third quarter in an incredible :22 4/5, she devoured the ground separating her and Winning Colors as Sham Say fell back.

Winning Colors reached the top of the stretch two lengths in front. Personal Ensign had all the momentum, but Winning Colors had the class to battle her the rest of the way, even as her lead shrunk to a half-length and then vanished as Personal Ensign stuck a head in front just past the eighth pole.

And still, Winning Colors found more.

Announcer Marshall Cassidy called, "Winning Colors won't give up; is coming on again!"

Until the final fifty yards, Winning Colors was within a head of her undefeated rival, but Personal Ensign inched away to a three-quarter-length margin at the wire, getting the mile in 1:34 1/5.

Stevens thought he was home free. "I thought she was a winner going down the stretch," he said. "When the other mare came to her, she really dug in and

really tried hard. I would have to mark this as one of her best races. I'm a little upset she ran that good and didn't win, but the other mare is a superstar."

Romero marveled at his unbeaten superstar: "To catch a horse running along on her own like she did...it's just very, very good. She's still number one."

Personal Ensign was eleven for eleven, with two dances left. She would make her final New York appearance at her favorite track, Belmont Park, in the grade I Beldame Stakes on October 16, then head to Churchill Downs for the Breeders' Cup Distaff.

Racing at a mile and a quarter and carrying co-high weight of 123 pounds against four rivals, Personal Ensign went off at 1-10 in the Beldame. Romero bided his time in third for three-quarters of a mile, then went after front-running Sham Say on the turn and collared her at the top of the stretch. Personal Ensign cruised home to a five and a half-length win in 2:01 1/5 over Classic Crown. "You can wait and make good decisions because she's so much better than these," Romero said. "You wait all your life to have something like her."

Personal Ensign and her perfect record were heading for Louisville, but she was not going alone.

PERSONAL ENSIGN

# CHAPTER 11

## *Perfection?*

Ogden Phipps' Personal Ensign would have been the envy of any racing stable, but her trainer, Shug McGaughey, was walking into the 1988 Breeders' Cup at Churchill Downs with a full house.

His other Breeders' Cup contenders were Dinny Phipps' unbeaten Mining, who would test his six-for-six record as the 8-5 favorite in the Sprint; the elder Phipps' rising two-year-old star Easy Goer; and Classic contenders Seeking the Gold and Personal Flag. That entry would face Alysheba, who had emerged as the lone horse who could derail Personal Ensign's Horse of the Year ambitions without facing her on the racetrack.

Few trainers have come to the Breeders' Cup so well armed since racing's championship day was inaugurated in 1984, and McGaughey felt the strain, particularly with it being Personal Ensign's final race.

"Being around her and having her has been an experience that I won't forget, but it's not all an experience that I'm going to miss when she's gone, because there's been a lot of pressure," McGaughey told reporters before the Distaff.

Racing of this caliber deserved a better backdrop than what the horses, horsemen, and a Breeders' Cup-record 71,237 fans had to endure that cold, damp, and dreary day in Louisville, an afternoon that concluded so close to evening that Churchill Downs officials had to turn on spotlights so people could see the final drama of the Breeders' Cup Classic unfold.

The Sprint, Distaff, Juvenile, and Classic were the fourth, sixth, eighth, and tenth races on the day's card, which included several non-Breeders' Cup races. The spacing allowed McGaughey to make four trips between Barn 42 on the Churchill backside and the track, which the previous night's rain had turned into a quagmire. The track condition was listed as sloppy for the first Breeders' Cup race, the Sprint, and was muddy the rest of the day.

McGaughey arrived at the barn at 6:15 that morning carrying a cup of coffee. He skipped breakfast, as usual.

The grooms cleaned the stalls of the five Phipps runners and then wrapped thick bandages around each horse's legs. Five black-and-red blankets were folded neatly over the slat in the barn door. Someone placed a muzzle on Mining to keep him out of his feed. Personal Ensign was restless in her stall. "She knew early something was going on," McGaughey's foreman, Tony Reinstedler, said. "She's smarter than we are."

In the late morning, McGaughey got into his maroon Cadillac and headed out to his condominium to change. Before heading back, his two-year-old son, Chip, said, "Good luck, Dad." McGaughey later told a friend, Dr. Mark Cheney, "That almost made me cry."

The late morning hours on race day always seem interminably long. This gloomy day, they seemed even longer at the McGaughey barn.

Mining stood with his forelegs in a bucket of ice for an hour to help a bad ankle. McGaughey walked to Personal Ensign's stall door and patted her nose. And waited. They both waited.

Finally, the announcer called the horses to the paddock for the Sprint.

Mining had beaten Gulch by two and three-quarter

lengths in taking the grade I Vosburgh Stakes at Belmont Park.

But in the Sprint, Gulch, benefiting from a masterful ride by Angel Cordero Jr., edged Play The King by three-quarters of a length, giving trainer D. Wayne Lukas a Breeders' Cup victory. Mining was tenth in the field of thirteen under Randy Romero, about eight lengths behind the winner.

"He didn't like the track," McGaughey tersely told a reporter after bringing Mining back to the barn. The escalating tension of the afternoon obviously was getting to him. "I don't want to answer any more questions now. I'm working."

Mining's defeat and the miserable weather blanketed the barn in gloom. "It was cold and very wet and very quiet," McGaughey's exercise rider, Dave Carroll, said. "Shug is very serious around the barn anyway. We were like, 'Jesus, it was going to be one of those days.' "

Personal Ensign's exercise rider, Lena Eriksson, felt it, too. "It was tense. There was a lot of pressure."

Yet with three more races ahead, McGaughey didn't have time to brood. He prepared Personal Ensign for her race and then accompanied her to the paddock for the last time. As the fillies walked onto the track for the post parade, the rain suddenly stopped.

The race had one of the most talent-laden fields ever assembled for the Distaff. In addition to Personal Ensign, it included Winning Colors and Goodbye Halo, who had won three consecutive grade I stakes.

After her brave defeat in the Maskette, Winning Colors had prepped for the Breeders' Cup in the grade I Spinster Stakes at Keeneland. Sent off in that race as the 3-10 favorite in a field of just five, she fought on the lead early and tired badly, finishing fourth, fifteen lengths behind long shot Hail a Cab. Goodbye Halo, meanwhile, had finished third in her most recent start, the grade II Las Palmas Handicap. Of the two of them, McGaughey judged Winning Colors as the filly to beat in the Distaff.

Coupled with Classic Crown, Winning Colors was the 4-1 second choice; Goodbye Halo, the 5-1 third choice. Personal Ensign, spotting Winning Colors and Goodbye Halo four pounds while carrying 123, went off as the favorite at 1-2.

In between the Sprint and the Distaff, D. Wayne Lukas had saddled his second Breeders' Cup winner of

the day. Eugene Klein's Open Mind, part of a five-horse Lukas entry in the Juvenile Fillies, led a one-two-three Lukas finish for three different owners. Already Lukas was hoping for a training triple as Winning Colors entered the starting gate in post-position eight. Personal Ensign had the six post and Goodbye Halo, ridden by Eddie Delahoussaye, the two.

As the horses loaded, announcer Tom Durkin, who was also calling the race for NBC, said, "Personal Ensign has taken her place in the starting gate, and she will certainly take her place in history as one of the greatest fillies of all time as she seeks to retire here undefeated, the first major American horse to do so in eighty years."

Romero couldn't help but hear. "I heard Tom Durkin saying she'd be the only filly in history to go undefeated, and I wanted to crawl underneath the gate," Romero said. "I said, 'All the world's on my shoulders.' "

The gates clanged open at 3:18 p.m.

On the track where she had won the Kentucky Derby wire to wire, Winning Colors bounced right to the lead under Gary Stevens. Personal Ensign broke seventh in between horses and then was floated wide on the first turn by Sham Say, a 30-1 long shot ridden by Jacinto Vasquez. "She broke well, but they out-footed her," Romero said. "Then Jacinto Vasquez hung me up pretty bad on the first turn. I was coming around [Sham Say]. I didn't want to be out that far. It developed that way."

Personal Ensign settled in sixth but was not handling the track. Dinny Phipps said afterward, "She looked like she was on skates. She just couldn't get hold of the track."

Romero knew he and his filly were in serious trouble over the deep and muddy track surface. "With Churchill Downs, you either like it or you don't," he said. "She was struggling to keep up."

Winning Colors had quickly opened a two and a half-length lead through an untaxing first quarter in :24 1/5. As she controlled the pace, she maintained a two and a half-length lead through a half-mile in :47 4/5 and kept the same margin in front of Goodbye Halo, who had rallied past Sham Say into second, after three quarters in 1:12. Winning Colors figured to have plenty left.

Personal Ensign, still sixth on the backstretch, had been taken to the inside by Romero and trailed by eight lengths in fifth with just a half-mile left in the race.

Romero had hoped to save ground, but he recognized his mistake. The filly continued to struggle on the gooey surface, and Romero couldn't get her comfortable. "What do I do now?" he wondered desperately.

Ogden Phipps thought it was hopeless. "I've run her in the damn Breeders' Cup race and broken her record of being unbeaten," he said to himself.

McGaughey, watching the race with his friend, Rogers Beasley, said, "Not today. She's beaten."

Assistant trainer Buzz Tenney was thinking, "This isn't the way this is supposed to end."

Tenney was right.

Romero hit Personal Ensign left-handed. She veered to the outside, finally discovering what she had been desperate to find the entire race: firm footing underneath her.

Now all she had to do was catch the Kentucky Derby winner six lengths in front of her.

Although Romero endured moments of desperation, "I never did give up on her. I always believed she was a champion, and I rode her that way. But I was very scared. I'd be lying if I told you I wasn't," he acknowledged.

"I found harder ground and she came running, and the filly in front of me was coming back."

Gradually, Personal Ensign cut into Winning Colors' lead.

The crowd had sensed Goodbye Halo gaining on the outside of Winning Colors, but now everyone realized Personal Ensign was gaining ground on both of them, as Romero hit her right-handed. Stevens countered by using his left hand repeatedly on Winning Colors.

"Here comes Personal Ensign unleashing a furious run!" Durkin yelled.

With a hundred yards left, Personal Ensign edged past Goodbye Halo. And still Winning Colors looked safe.

Twenty yards from the wire, Personal Ensign drew even with the front-runner. And one last time, Personal Ensign surged forward.

"The last two jumps I hand rode her," Romero said. "I put my stick away. There was no more whipping. It wasn't helping her anymore. I said I wasn't going to override her."

Personal Ensign and Winning Colors crossed the finish line together in 1:52 for the mile and an eighth. Goodbye Halo was in between them, just a half-length back.

The roar of the crowd was deafening. Many, including Ogden and Dinny Phipps, who were sitting a hundred yards in front of the finish line, were uncertain who had won.

Romero knew.

Passing Lena Eriksson, on her pony at the seven-eighths pole, he told her, "We got it."

Upstairs in the clubhouse Dr. Larry Bramlage, who had fixed her broken pastern, watched the Distaff with Churchill Downs chairman Warner Jones. "When she came around the turn into the stretch, I, like everybody else, was preparing myself for her to lose the race," Bramlage said. "Then she kept coming and coming. When she crossed the finish line, everybody took a collective deep breath. It was sort of surreal, like a dream for her to finish like that."

On NBC Dick Enberg gave his best, "Oh, my!" An outrider with a microphone rode over to Personal Ensign as Romero pulled her up on the backstretch.

Enberg asked Romero whether he had won, and he

said yes. Asked his thoughts at this moment, Romero said softly, "I've always dreamed of having an undefeated horse. I'm glad it's over."

He sounded exhausted, and he was after a brilliant ride. "I had pulled all the strength out of my body because I was trying to get her there and it wasn't happening," he said. Yet it did, and Romero's ride was crucial.

As Enberg continued his questions, the result was made official, and Churchill Downs vibrated with the response. The outrider yelled to Romero, "You've got it! You're in, brother!"

McGaughey was stunned. "I thought she was hopelessly beaten," he said. Instead, Personal Ensign had won by a nose. McGaughey had done it. He had crafted her perfect career: thirteen for thirteen.

Lukas, a former high school basketball coach, likened Winning Colors' defeat to getting beaten by a thirty-foot jumper at the buzzer, but immediately congratulated McGaughey after the race.

Groom Terry Cooney led Personal Ensign in circles as everyone waited for the ceremony in the winner's circle. She was crying quietly, as was nearly everyone else associated with the filly.

Romero was shaking when the ceremony finally got under way. He hugged McGaughey and said, "Can you believe this?" McGaughey replied, "I thought she was beat." Romero responded, "She's a fighter."

Romero was, too. "I give Randy a lot of credit for that ride, for all his rides on her, because there was a lot of pressure," Eriksson said. "He knew her well. He kept cool and didn't panic."

Romero allowed himself a smile. "It was the happiest moment of my life," he said. "I will never forget that day."

Kentucky Governor Martha Layne Collins presented the winning trophy to the Phippses, but McGaughey did not have time to savor the moment. He had to get Easy Goer prepared for the Juvenile, and Seeking the Gold and Personal Flag for the Classic.

Easy Goer, a son of Alydar out of Relaxing by Buckpasser, had followed a nose loss in his debut by winning a maiden, allowance, and two grade I stakes, the Cowdin and Champagne. The odds-on favorite, he did not win the Breeders' Cup Juvenile, rallying from ninth in the field of ten to finish second by a length and a quarter to Is It True, a 9-1 longshot owned by Eugene

Klein, trained by Lukas, and ridden superbly by Laffit Pincay Jr., who would become racing's all-time leading jockey. Easy Goer did not help his chances by jumping the tracks left by the starting gate as he made his rally.

Personal Ensign was a lock for an Eclipse Award for older female and would have been the 1988 Horse of the Year in a landslide had Alysheba not won the Classic. McGaughey had two shots to beat the 1987 Kentucky Derby winner with Personal Flag and Seeking the Gold. Personal Flag was sixth in the field of nine, but Seeking the Gold nearly got the job done. Rallying strongly from seventh under Pat Day, Seeking the Gold got within a head of Alysheba at the top of the stretch. The two fought it out to the wire, with Alysheba and jockey Chris McCarron gamely holding on by a half-length. The victory was Alysheba's fourth straight, following wins in three other grade I stakes, the Iselin, Woodward, and Meadowlands Cup, and made him seven for nine for the year. In winning the Classic, Alysheba passed John Henry as racing's all-time leading money earner with $6,679,242. Alysheba would be named Horse of the Year by a wide margin.

After the Classic, McGaughey walked back to the

barn with trainer Charlie Whittingham, whose long-shot in the Classic, Lively One, had finished eighth.

It was cold and dark and spitting snow.

"How'd you do?" asked Whittingham.

"I won one and had two good seconds," said McGaughey.

"You had a good day," the master trainer replied.

"That picked my head up," McGaughey said twelve years later. "I was young then. I thought I was supposed to win every one."

He had won the one he wanted most.

"There was a sense of relief," McGaughey said. "I knew she was going home. I knew she was going home undefeated."

# PERSONAL ENSIGN

## EPILOGUE

## *The Kids*

Millions of television viewers watched Personal Ensign's remarkable determination in the 1988 Distaff, a race many call the greatest in Breeders' Cup history. But only a handful of people can testify that she did not leave her indomitable will on the racetrack.

"I was here the day she came back from the racetrack," Gus Koch, assistant manager of Claiborne Farm, said. "She didn't want to be fooled around with. Wouldn't let the blacksmith take her shoes off. She's tough."

She proved how tough ten years later, almost dying while trying to deliver a foal in 1998. "She had what we call a dystocia, a difficult labor, when she lost a Mr. Prospector foal," Koch said. "She had a tear in her uterus and peritonitis, a severe infection in her abdomen, which can be fatal. She was a very sick mare.

"It took a lot of time and a couple of surgeries. Then she had a post-surgery condition. We just felt that if it was an ordinary mare...It took her better than a year to recover. She was in a lot of distress.

"If she hadn't so much heart, we would have lost her."

That would have been quite a loss. For Personal Ensign, the 1996 Kentucky Broodmare of the Year, has passed on her ability to her foals, producing Miner's Mark, Our Emblem, Pennant Champion, My Flag, Proud and True, and Traditionally, all winners, who have aggregate earnings of more than $3.4 million. My Flag, Miner's Mark, and Traditionally have accounted for the majority of that purse money and six grade I stakes victories by themselves.

All have been born at Claiborne Farm, birthplace of Personal Ensign and most of the Phipps champions. Claiborne encompasses some 3,000 acres outside of Paris, Kentucky, and is steeped in history and tradition. Secretariat; his sire, Bold Ruler; Mr. Prospector; Buckpasser; Gallant Fox; Hoist the Flag; Nasrullah; Nijinsky II; Princequillo; Riva Ridge; Round Table; Swale; and a host of other equine luminaries have inhabited the paddocks and old barns and imprinted their greatness on subsequent generations.

It was here that Personal Ensign eased into a second career. Meanwhile, jockey Randy Romero, trainer Shug McGaughey, and owner Ogden Phipps continued their incredible roll.

Romero finished 1989 as the thirteenth leading rider in the country with a little more than $6.6 million in earnings. His 171 victories included three grade I stakes, the Breeders' Cup Juvenile Fillies with Go for Wand, who was also second in the grade I Frizette to Stella Madrid; the Vosburgh on Sewickley; and the Blue Grass Stakes on Western Playboy.

Romero rode Go for Wand in all of her starts. Owned by Christiana Stable and trained by Billy Badgett, the filly was the 1989 champion of her division. In her first eight starts at three, she was nearly perfect, with seven stakes victories and a second in the grade I Kentucky Oaks.

She entered the starting gate for the 1990 Breeders' Cup Distaff at Belmont Park with a lifetime record of ten victories and two seconds in twelve starts. She did not survive the race. Straining to protect a slim lead against the top mare Bayakoa, Go for Wand shattered her right ankle, pitching Romero to the track. She then tried to get up and finish the race before collapsing at the finish line. She was euthanized.

Romero suffered eight fractured ribs and a hairline fracture of his shoulder in that spill. Yet he rode Izvestia in the three-million-dollar Breeders' Cup Classic later that afternoon, finishing sixth, ten lengths behind Unbridled.

Three and a half months after Go for Wand's accident, just days into his comeback, Romero broke his left elbow and left collarbone in an accident at Gulfstream Park. His career was never the same. "My career never got to its fullest," he said. "It never affected my riding, but I could never get back to the top."

He never stopped trying, though, even riding for a short time in Hong Kong. He finally retired July 12, 1999, and was honored at Evangeline Downs in Lafayette, Louisiana, where he had first risen to prominence. He won 4,294 races, more than $75.2 million dollars, and rode two of the greatest fillies of the twentieth century.

In 1989, the year after Personal Ensign retired, Ogden Phipps led the country in earnings by an owner.

Phipps' runners had twenty-five wins and earnings of $5,438,034, with stable star Easy Goer leading the cavalcade. The son of Alydar came within a neck of giving the Phipps family three Breeders' Cup winners in one glorious afternoon at Gulfstream Park. First, Ogden Phipps' Dancing Spree, a 16-1 longshot under Angel Cordero Jr., edged Safely Kept by a neck to win the Sprint. Dinny Phipps' Rhythm won the Juvenile by two lengths under Craig Perret. Then, in the Classic, Easy Goer faced off with year-long rival Sunday Silence and lost by a neck, costing him Horse of the Year and divisional championship honors.

Ogden Phipps was also 1989's leading breeder with more than $5.5 million in earnings. He continued to breed and race stakes winners through the nineties and into the twenty-first century, including Heavenly Prize, the 1994 champion three-year-old filly.

Shug McGaughey's career after Personal Ensign has been marked by highs and lows. He ended 1989 as the nation's third-leading trainer in earnings with $8.3 million, trailing only D. Wayne Lukas and Charlie Whittingham. In doing so, McGaughey won fifty-five of 178 starts, producing an unfathomable win percent-

age of 30.9 for an entire year, a percentage he matched in 1994 winning eighty of 258 starts. The average winning percentage for all trainers is eleven percent.

While his training career continued to flourish, his personal life spiraled downward. He endured the death of his father and a crumbling marriage to Mary Jane, the mother of his sons Chip and Reeve, that would end in divorce in 1991. In the early 1990s, McGaughey took time off from training for personal reasons. "I was just kind of confused," McGaughey said. "My marriage wasn't going good. My father died. I was kind of getting out of hand."

Still, his horses won sixty-three races and more than three million dollars in 1991, and fifty-one races and more than four million dollars in 1992.

In 1993 McGaughey's career peaked with an unprecedented five stakes wins on October 16, Breeders' Cup Preview Day at Belmont Park. He won the Jockey Club Gold Cup with Personal Ensign's first foal, Miner's Mark, the Kelso Handicap with Lure, the Frizette with Heavenly Prize, the Beldame with Dispute, and the Lawrence Realization with Strolling Along.

McGaughey enjoyed success with two top fillies in

1995, when Inside Information won the Breeders' Cup Distaff at Belmont Park and Heavenly Prize finished second. That same day a problematic filly named My Flag won the Breeders' Cup Juvenile Fillies.

After that year, McGaughey had mixed success, winning "only" forty-two races and $2.9 million in 1987, but sixty-two races and more than $5 million in '98, behind temperamental Coronado's Quest, who won the Wood Memorial, Riva Ridge, Dwyer, Haskell, and the Travers.

"I'm not as happy the last five years," McGaughey said early in 2001. "It's disappointing to me to go to Gulfstream Park on Florida Derby Day and have a horse running in the fourth race. It's disappointing that we haven't been competitive on Breeders' Cup Day."

After Personal Ensign, it would be difficult for any champion to measure up. And while motherhood may have mellowed Personal Ensign, she retains the same fire she displayed on the racetrack. "She's very independent, very strong-willed," Koch said. "This mare doesn't want you to feed her carrots. This mare, she's nobody's pet."

Lena Eriksson, Personal Ensign's former exercise rider, tries to see the mare every year that her job

brings her to nearby Keeneland. "She's very unsociable," she said. "I came out to see her after she had My Flag. I came out there walking with Dell Hancock. She nickered to her baby and walked off. She didn't want us to bother her. You're not going to pet her."

Yet her maternal instincts are strong.

"She raises a big, healthy, strong foal, and I mean she raises it, too," Seth Hancock told *Daily Racing Form.* "She works at it. When she's out in the field, she keeps an eye on that foal. Not that she's nasty with other mares or foals, but if they get to fooling with her baby, then they've got problems. She won't hurt one of them, but she'll make damn sure they know they'd better go somewhere else."

Personal Ensign was bred to Mr. Prospector the first three years. Her first Mr. Prospector foal, Miner's Mark, born February 15, 1990, won six of eighteen starts, including the grade I Jockey Club Gold Cup, grade II Jim Dandy Stakes, and grade III Colin Stakes, and earned $967,170. Miner's Mark entered stud at Lane's End Farm in Versailles, Kentucky in 1995, and later was moved to Florida.

Miner's Mark represented "a perfect cross" of Personal

Ensign and Mr. Prospector, which is why Hancock paired them for two additional years. "We wouldn't normally do something like that, but he seemed like he was the right horse when she came here," Hancock told the *Form*.

On March 7, 1991, Personal Ensign produced Our Emblem, who posted five firsts, five seconds, and five thirds in twenty-seven career starts, earning $366,013. Though Our Emblem did not win a stakes, he was second in the grade I Carter and grade II Tom Fool and Forego handicaps, and third in the grade I Vosburgh and Metropolitan handicaps, grade II Commonwealth Breeders' Cup, and grade III Gulfstream Park Breeders' Cup Sprint Championship and Westchester Handicap.

Personal Ensign's third foal was a filly, Pennant Champion, foaled March 15, 1992. She started just seven times, winning twice and making $48,070.

Hancock and the Phippses then sent Personal Ensign to the Phipps' homebred champion Easy Goer. On March 25, 1993, the same year she was elected to the Racing Hall of Fame, Personal Ensign produced a filly, My Flag.

My Flag would test McGaughey's patience, knowledge, and dedication and reward him handsomely. At two, after placing in the Matron and Frizette, she doggedly wore down Cara Rafaela, trained by D. Wayne Lukas, to win the 1995 Breeders' Cup Juvenile Fillies by a half-length at Belmont Park, making Personal Ensign the first mare ever to win a Breeders' Cup race and produce a Breeders' Cup winner.

My Flag's victory in the Juvenile Fillies, however, was only her second in six starts. "She's been such a difficult project mentally," McGaughey told *The Blood-Horse* after the race.

My Flag was at her worst walking from the barn to the paddock before a race. "She would turn herself inside out," McGaughey said. "She would buck, turn sideways, and kick at the crowd. She was getting so wound up that I thought it was taking away any chance she had to really run her race."

McGaughey tried calming My Flag by putting cotton in her ears, but that didn't work. So he began schooling her in the paddocks in the afternoon, a procedure he'd used once or twice to calm other nervous horses. With My Flag, McGaughey estimated that she had fifty sessions. "That may be an exaggeration, but there were a lot of them," he said.

In the Frizette, her last start before the Breeders' Cup,

McGaughey added blinkers. My Flag ran a strong second by three-quarters of a length to Golden Attraction, the Lukas-trained filly who would be made the favorite in the Juvenile Fillies. My Flag would be second choice at 7-2.

My Flag's pre-race itinerary included McGaughey's stable pony, Levi, standing in front of her stall to block out the crowd in the paddock and exclusion from the post parade. It worked as My Flag closed from next-to-last to win the million-dollar race.

At three My Flag would win three more grade I stakes, the Ashland, Coaching Club American Oaks, and Gazelle, as well as the grade II Bonnie Miss Stakes. She also finished third in the Belmont Stakes against colts.

My Flag ended her career with six wins, three seconds, and four thirds from twenty starts and earnings of $1,557,057. Retired to Claiborne like her mother, My Flag produced her first foal, a filly by Storm Cat named On Parade, on January 28, 1999.

Due to My Flag's accomplishments, Personal Ensign was named 1996 Kentucky Broodmare of the Year, the seventh Phipps family mare to be so honored since their Bloodroot won the first award fifty years earlier.

Personal Ensign's fifth foal, a Mr. Prospector colt

named Proud and True, was born April 4, 1994, and won three of nine starts and $96,170.

The champion mare had been turning out winners with uncanny precision, but then produced just one foal between 1995 and 1999: Traditionally.

Personal Ensign was bred twice to Seeking the Gold and aborted both times. So in 1996, she was once again bred to Mr. Prospector, foaling Traditionally the following April. He showed potential as a two-year-old, winning his second start, but finished a distant sixth to Greenwood Lake in the 1999 Champagne Stakes. Traditionally bounced back to win an allowance race by two lengths, then tried Greenwood Lake again in the Remsen, finishing a respectable fifth to him in the field of eight, beaten just three and a half lengths.

In 2000 Traditionally finished third in an allowance race, then ran last of twelve at 88-1 in the Wood Memorial behind Fusaichi Pegasus, who went on to win the Kentucky Derby.

McGaughey tried Traditionally on grass and the colt only placed once in four starts. His three-year-old season was over and he had just two thirds and earnings of $15,640 to show for his six starts.

So what was he doing in a grade I stakes the following spring?

McGaughey was confident he had finally figured Traditionally out and paired the challenging colt with new rider Pat Day. His instructions: ride with sensitive hands. "I knew Traditionally didn't want his mouth messed with," the trainer said. McGaughey was rewarded when Traditionally won two allowance races, then took the Oaklawn Handicap convincingly.

McGaughey allowed himself to enjoy this victory. "(Shug) can win a race, and sometimes it's not good enough," said Allison McGaughey, who married McGaughey in 1997. "I get excited and want to high-five him, and he's worrying about where the horse is going to race next. He's very intense. He smiles and laughs, but when he's at work, he's all business. The day of the race, it could be the Breeders' Cup or an allowance race, if he's got his game face on, I stay out of his way."

Other stables might have given up on Traditionally. McGaughey and Ogden Phipps did not, and now Personal Ensign has another grade I stakes winner.

Following Personal Ensign's brush with death, she was not bred in 1998. She was bred the following

season to A.P. Indy, and foaled a filly named Possibility on April 25, 2000. Personal Ensign was barren after being bred to Unbridled in 2000, and was bred back to him on April 8, 2001 and pronounced in foal.

Personal Ensign clearly has left a tough, if not impossible, act for her progeny to follow. "The longer I'm around racehorses, the more amazed I am that she went to the post thirteen times and didn't have a single bad day," Dr. Larry Bramlage said.

She could have that cold and rainy afternoon at Churchill Downs, but she refused to give in. Her last lunge in the last race of her career to edge Winning Colors will forever remind us that Personal Ensign was not only a champion. She was an undefeated champion.

| | | | Sunglow |
| | | Sword Dancer, 1956 | Highland Fling |
| | Damascus, 1964 | | |
| | | Kerala, 1958 | My Babu |
| PRIVATE ACCOUNT, | | | Blade of Time |
| b, 1976 | | | |
| | | Buckpasser, 1963 | Tom Fool |
| | | | Busanda |
| | Numbered Account, 1969 | | |
| PERSONAL ENSIGN, | | Intriguing, 1964 | Swaps |
| bay filly, | | | Glamour |
| 1984 | | | |
| | | Tom Rolfe, 1962 | Ribot |
| | | | Pocahontas |
| | Hoist the Flag, 1968 | | |
| | | Wavy Navy, 1954 | War Admiral |
| GRECIAN BANNER, | | | Triomphe |
| dkb/br, 1974 | | | |
| | | Aristophanes, 1948 | Hyperion |
| | | | Commotion |
| | Dorine, 1958 | | |
| | | Doria, 1949 | Advocate |
| | | | Donatila |

# PERSONAL ENSIGN's RACE RECORD

## Personal Ensign

**b. f. 1984, by Private Account (Damascus)–Grecian Banner, by Hoist the Flag**

**Lifetime record: 13 13 0 0 $1,679,880**

**Own.– Ogden Phipps**
**Br.– Ogden Phipps (Ky)**
**Tr.– Claude McGaughey III**

| | | | | | | | | | | | | | | | | | | |
|---|---|---|---|---|---|---|---|---|---|---|---|---|---|---|---|---|---|---|
| 5Nov88- 6CD | my 1⅛ | $:47^{4}$ | 1:12 | $1:38^{1}$ | 1:52 | 3↑ Ⓕ BC Distaff-G1 | 6 | 6 | $5^{8\frac{1}{2}}$ | $5^{8}$ | $3^{4}$ | $1^{no}$ | Romero RP | 123 | *.50 | 82-20 | Personal Ensign$123^{no}$Winning Colors$119\frac{1}{2}$Goodbye Halo$119^{5}$ | 9 |
| | Tight early,just up | | | | | | | | | | | | | | | | | |
| 16Oct88- 8Bel | fst 1¼ | $:48^{1}$ | 1:12 | $1:36^{2}$ | $2:01^{1}$ | 3↑ Ⓕ Beldame-G1 | 1 | 3 | $2^{2}$ | $2^{hd}$ | $1^{2}$ | $1^{5\frac{1}{2}}$ | Romero RP | 123 | *.10 | 92-16 | PersonlEnsign$123^{5\frac{1}{2}}$ClassicCrown$118\frac{1}{2}$ShmSy$118^{7}$ Ridden out | 5 |
| 10Sep88- 8Bel | fst 1 | $:22^{4}$ | $:45^{1}$ | 1:09 | $1:34^{1}$ | 3↑ Ⓕ Maskette-G1 | 2 | 3 | $3^{6}$ | $2^{2}$ | $2^{hd}$ | $1^{\frac{3}{4}}$ | Romero RP | 123 | *.30 | 94-14 | PersonalEnsgn$123\frac{3}{4}$WinningColrs$118^{5\frac{1}{4}}$ShmSy$115^{11\frac{1}{4}}$ Driving | 4 |
| 6Aug88- 8Sar | sly 1⅛ | $:47^{2}$ | $1:11^{3}$ | $1:35^{3}$ | $1:47^{4}$ | 3↑ Whitney H-G1 | 3 | 3 | $3^{3}$ | $2^{1}$ | $1^{hd}$ | $1^{1\frac{1}{2}}$ | Romero RP | 117 | *.80 | 96-12 | PersonalEnsign$117^{1\frac{1}{2}}$Gulch$124^{17}$King'sSwan123 Brisk urging | 3 |
| 4Jly88-10Mth | fst 1$\frac{1}{16}$ | :24 | $:47^{2}$ | $1:10^{4}$ | $1:41^{4}$ | 3↑ Ⓕ Molly Pitcher H-G2 | 5 | 3 | $2^{3}$ | $2\frac{1}{2}$ | $1^{2\frac{1}{2}}$ | $1^{8}$ | Romero RP | 125 | *.40 | 96-14 | Personal Ensign$125^{8}$Grecian Flight$119^{7}$Le L'Argent$117^{1}$ | 5 |
| | Bumped,forced wide | | | | | | | | | | | | | | | | | |
| 11Jun88- 7Bel | fst 1⅛ | $:47^{1}$ | $1:11^{2}$ | $1:35^{3}$ | $1:47^{3}$ | 3↑ Ⓕ Hempstead H-G1 | 5 | 3 | $3^{1\frac{1}{2}}$ | $3^{1}$ | $1^{4}$ | $1^{7}$ | Romero RP | 123 | *.40 | 89-13 | PersonlEnsgn$123^{7}$HomtwnQun$109^{2}$ClbbrGrl$118^{nk}$ Ridden out | 5 |
| 15May88- 8Bel | fst 1$\frac{1}{16}$ | :23 | $:45^{3}$ | 1:10 | $1:41^{3}$ | 3↑ Ⓕ Shuvee H-G1 | 5 | 3 | $3^{3}$ | $2^{hd}$ | $1\frac{1}{2}$ | $1^{1\frac{3}{4}}$ | Romero RP | 121 | *.70 | 94-15 | Personal Ensign$121^{1\frac{3}{4}}$Clabber Girl$118^{3\frac{1}{4}}$Bishop's Delight$111^{2\frac{3}{4}}$ | 6 |
| | Driving | | | | | | | | | | | | | | | | | |
| 18Oct87- 8Bel | fst 1¼ | $:49^{3}$ | $1:13^{4}$ | $1:38^{2}$ | $2:04^{2}$ | 3↑ Ⓕ Beldame-G1 | 8 | 2 | $2\frac{1}{2}$ | $1^{3}$ | $1^{4}$ | $1^{2\frac{1}{4}}$ | Romero RP | 118 | 1.30 | 76-23 | PersnlEnsgn$118^{2\frac{1}{4}}$CoupdFusl$123^{2\frac{1}{2}}$SlntTurn$118^{3\frac{3}{4}}$ Drew clear | 10 |
| 10Oct87- 5Bel | fst 1 | $:22^{3}$ | $:45^{4}$ | $1:10^{2}$ | $1:36^{3}$ | Ⓕ Rare Perfume-G2 | 2 | 3 | $1^{1}$ | $1^{5}$ | $1^{5}$ | $1^{4\frac{3}{4}}$ | Romero RP | 115 | *.80 | 82-22 | PrsnlEnsign$115^{4\frac{3}{4}}$OneFromHevn$118^{3\frac{3}{4}}$KyBd$118^{1\frac{1}{2}}$ Ridden out | 9 |
| 24Sep87- 5Bel | fst 1 | $:23^{3}$ | $:46^{4}$ | $1:11^{3}$ | $1:36^{1}$ | 3↑ Ⓕ Alw 33000 | 5 | 2 | $1^{2\frac{1}{2}}$ | $1^{3}$ | $1^{5}$ | $1^{7\frac{3}{4}}$ | Romero RP | 113 | *.20 | 84-20 | PersonalEnsign$113^{7\frac{3}{4}}$WithaTwist$117^{nk}$RosaMay$117^{6}$ Handily | 5 |
| 6Sep87- 5Bel | fst 7f | $:23^{2}$ | $:46^{2}$ | $1:10^{3}$ | $1:23^{1}$ | 3↑ Ⓕ Alw 31000 | 3 | 5 | $4^{3}$ | $1^{hd}$ | $1^{1\frac{1}{2}}$ | $1^{3\frac{3}{4}}$ | Bailey JD | 113 | *.70 | 86-19 | PersonalEnsign$113^{3\frac{3}{4}}$ChicShirine$113^{1\frac{1}{4}}$WithTwst$117\frac{1}{2}$ Handily | 6 |
| 13Oct86- 8Bel | fst 1 | $:23^{2}$ | :46 | $1:10^{1}$ | $1:36^{2}$ | Ⓕ Frizette-G1 | 2 | 2 | $2\frac{1}{2}$ | $2^{hd}$ | $1^{hd}$ | $1^{hd}$ | Romero RP | 119 | *.30 | 83-16 | PersonalEnsign$119^{hd}$Collins$119^{5\frac{1}{2}}$FlyingKatuna119 Driving | 3 |
| 28Sep86- 6Bel | my 7f | $:23^{1}$ | $:46^{3}$ | $1:10^{3}$ | $1:22^{4}$ | Ⓕ Md Sp Wt | 5 | 7 | $2^{2\frac{1}{2}}$ | $1^{1\frac{1}{2}}$ | $1^{7}$ | $1^{12\frac{3}{4}}$ | Romero RP | 117 | *.90 | 88-15 | Personal Ensign$117^{12\frac{3}{4}}$Graceful Darby$117^{2\frac{3}{4}}$Nastique$117^{1\frac{1}{2}}$ | 7 |
| | Hesitated start,clear | | | | | | | | | | | | | | | | | |

# Index

# Photo Credits

*Cover photo:* (Dan Johnson)

*Page 1:* Personal Ensign race shot, paddock shot (both Barbara D. Livingston)

*Page 2:* Private Account (Dell Hancock); Damascus (The Blood-Horse); Dorine (Turf Argentino); Hoist the Flag (The Blood-Horse); Personal Ensign foal shot (Courtesy of The Jockey Club)

*Page 3:* Gladys Livingston Mills Phipps (Morgan Photo Service); Dinny Phipps and Shug McGaughey, Ogden Phipps and Ogden Phipps II (both Anne M. Eberhardt)

*Page 4:* Shug McGaughey (Skip Dickstein); Buzz Tenney, Randy Romero (both Barbara D. Livingston); Terry Cooney with Personal Ensign (Anne M. Eberhardt)

*Page 5:* Personal Ensign winning the Frizette (Bob Coglianese); Dr. Larry Bramlage (Anne M. Eberhardt); Personal Ensign X-ray (Courtesy of Dr. Bramlage)

*Page 6:* Winning the Rare Perfume, Working out (both Barbara D. Livingston); Winning the Beldame (Bob Coglianese)

*Page 7:* Winning the Hempstead (Dan Johnson); Winning the Shuvee, After the Hempstead (both Bob Coglianese)

*Page 8-9:* Winning the Molly Pitcher (Bill Denver/Equi-Photo); In the paddock before Whitney (Barbara D. Livingston); Winning the Whitney (Skip Dickstein)

*Page 10:* The Maskette head on (Bob Coglianese); The Maskette side view (Barbara D. Livingston); Winning the 1988 Beldame (Bob Coglianese)

*Page 11:* Breeders' Cup Distaff post parade (Anne M. Eberhardt); Distaff finish inside rail (E. Martin Jessee); Distaff finish outside rail (Dan Johnson)

*Page 12:* Randy Romero and Personal Ensign post-Distaff (Dan Johnson); Terry Cooney and Personal Ensign post-Distaff (Skip Dickstein)

*Page 13:* Personal Ensign unloading from van, In Claiborne paddock (both Dell Hancock)

*Page 14:* Miner's Mark (NYRA); Personal Ensign with My Flag (Dell Hancock); My Flag (Barbara D. Livingston)

*Page 15:* Traditionally (Matt Goins/Equipix); Personal Ensign with Traditionally (Dell Hancock); Personal Ensign with Possibility (Cheryl Manista)

*Page 16:* Personal Ensign (Milt Toby); Hall of Fame ceremony (Barbara D. Livingston); Broodmare of the Year (Anne M. Eberhardt)

## ABOUT THE
# AUTHOR

B ill Heller, a freelance writer in Albany, New York, won the 1997 Eclipse Award for Magazine Writing for his story, "The Times They Are a-Changin'," in *The Backstretch* magazine. He also is a three-time winner of the John Hervey Award for Harness Racing Magazine Writing. Heller won the 1999 Bill Leggett Breeders' Cup magazine writing award and a 2000 writing award from the American Horse Publications. He currently writes for the *Thoroughbred Times, The Backstretch,* and *Mid-Atlantic Thoroughbred.*

Heller has authored eleven other books, including *Forego*: Thoroughbred Legends; *Go for Wand*: Thoroughbred Legends; *Obsession — Bill Musselman's Relentless Quest; Overlay, Overlay; The Will To Win — The Ron Turcotte Story; Travelin' Sam, America's Sports Ambassador; Billy Haughton — The Master;* and *Playing Tall — The 10 Shortest Players in NBA History.*

Forthcoming titles
in the

# THOROUGHBRED
# Legends®

series:

**Sunday Silence**

**Ruffian**

**Swaps**

**Affirmed/Alydar**

**Round Table**

*Available titles*

**Man o' War**

**Dr. Fager**

**Citation**

**Go for Wand**

**Seattle Slew**

**Forego**

**Native Dancer**

**Nashua**

**Spectacular Bid**

**John Henry**